THE INNER TEMPLE

MEDITATIONS
TO HEAL & INSPIRE

by

Hanne Jahr
Poems by Stephanie Sorréll

Science of Thought Press Ltd.

Bosham House, Bosham, Chichester, West Sussex PO18 8PJ
England

Telephone/Fax 01243-572109
email: scienceofthought@mistral.co.uk

First Published 1998

© Copyright: Hanne Jahr 1998
© Copyright illustrations: Hanne Jahr 1998
© Copyright poems: Stephanie Sorréll 1997 & 1998

Published by
The Science of Thought Press Ltd.
Bosham House
Bosham
Chichester
West Sussex PO18 8PJ
England

A catalogue record for this book
is available from the British Library
ISBN 0 9531597 1 X

Cover design and illustrations by Hanne Jahr

Typeset by Michael Walsh at MusicPrint
Chichester, West Sussex
Printed and bound by RPM Reprographics
Chichester, West Sussex

All rights reserved. No part of this publication may be reproduced, stored in a retrieval stystem, or transmited, in any form or by any means, electronic, mechanical, photocopying, recording or otherwise, without prior permission from the copyright holders.

DEDICATION

This book is dedicated to the two
contemporary mystics, Henry Thomas Hamblin and
Grace Cooke (and her teacher, White Eagle)
whose life works this book has grown out of,
and to the shining company in the world of light
whom they have now joined.

ACKNOWLEDGEMENTS

A special 'thank you' to Stephanie Sorréll for writing the introduction and for all the hours spent scanning and correcting the text and helping to edit the material. Thank you also for the contribution of poems and for your support in publishing this book, and for your loyal friendship.

I am also particularly grateful to Ylana Hayward for writing the foreword, but also for being a pillar of light and love in my life over the past 20 years.

I am also indebted to the White Eagle Publishing Trust for their generous permission to use the many quotes from their books. And to Jean LeFevre for letting me use the Stepping Stone meditation. Also, not least, to Marie Mares for proof reading.

CONTENTS

FOREWORD by Ylana Hayward 7

INTRODUCTION by Stephanie Sorréll 9

CHAPTER ONE : **The Inner Light** 11
   Your True Self and the Purpose of Meditation 13

CHAPTER TWO : **Preparing Yourself for Meditation** 17
   Closing Ritual 19
   Music and Inspirational Writings as Tools in Meditation 24

CHAPTER THREE : **Festivals (Our Inner Cycles)** 29

CHAPTER FOUR : **Finding a Teacher and Following the Heart** ... 34
   Finding a Teacher 34
   Meeting an Initiate 38
   Path of the Heart 42

CHAPTER FIVE : **Controlling Our Emotions** 48
   Practical Thought Control 52
   Overcoming Fear and Unwanted Thoughts 55

CHAPTER SIX: **Tests on the Path** 61

CHAPTER SEVEN : **Angels and Guardians** 67
   Angels 67
   Guardian Angels and Guardian Spirits 72

CHAPTER EIGHT : **Using Our Inner Senses to Create** *79*
   The Use of Scent as an Aid in Meditation *83*
   Colour *88*
   Path to the Great Silence (a Seneca Indian Meditation) *96*

CHAPTER NINE : **Crystals** *100*
   Introduction to the Quartz Crystals *105*

CHAPTER TEN : **Inner Communion** *108*
   Our Real Self and the Kingdom of Heaven *112*
   How Mystical Experiences and Meditation Can Help us
   in Our Daily Life. *117*

CHAPTER ELEVEN : **From Doing to Being** *121*
   Quietness Versus Negative Passivity. *125*

CHAPTER TWELVE : **Sounding Our True Note** *129*

EPILOGUE : **The Inner Temple** by Stephanie Sorréll *135*

FOREWORD

I feel grateful for having been asked to write the foreword to Hanne's beautiful book, for of course this could not be done until I had read it, and to do so has been a most uplifting and inspiring experience.

The book, *The Inner Temple*, has its origin in the series of meditations contributed by Hanne to the *Science of Thought Review* over several years. The meditations, without exception, are really beautiful; each one takes you gently and peacefully into the inner world; and Hanne's suggestion that the reader should read them onto a tape so that he or she can just relax and listen and see, rather than have to read, is an excellent idea which I warmly recommend.

Apart from the actual meditations given, the book is a helpful and sound guide to the art of creative meditation generally, and one of the joys of reading Hanne's writing is the blend of spiritual vision with sound commonsense and humour. She often quotes the saying, 'Feet on earth, head in heaven', and I think her writing is a demonstration of the wisdom of these words.

Each chapter contains helpful guidance on the various aspects of meditation, the lessons to be learned, the problems which can arise (such as the busy mind and emotions, and questions such as 'Who is my teacher? How can I find him or her? What is the difference between my guide and guardian angel? And the very special section on overcoming fear – a problem which, consciously or unconsciously, we all face.) One very special passage is where Hanne describes her meeting with the Dalai Lama – a perfect example for us all of a true brother and teacher.

I had an interesting experience while reading Hanne's suggestion about how to withdraw from disturbing sound. As I started to read, a helicopter arrived overhead and hovered there for some time, making an unspeakable noise, as helicopters will. However, I put Hanne's suggestion into practice and was able to withdraw totally from the sound and didn't even hear the machine fly off – a very valuable lesson which I will not forget!

Also, reading the section about colour, I found myself withdrawn from the world and embraced peacefully in a lovely rainbow, and filled with its light and colour.

Having said all this, for me the most beautiful section of the book – its essence really – is the chapter on inner communion. For me it encapsulates the whole purpose of meditation. As Hanne so rightly explains, creative visualisation is not an end in itself but rather a means to an end. The beautiful experiences she shares with us, the beauties of the world into which she gently leads us, all help to quieten the emotions and still the busy mind of every day (not easy in today's world) and to lead us gradually to find that place of deep and utter stillness in our own hearts, and in the heart of the universe. In a word, we find the 'jewel in the lotus of the heart', the Christ in us, and the God in all life.

May the jewel in our hearts radiate light and healing and love into all God's world.

Thank you, Hanne, for all you have shared with us; for the light and inspiration which shines through the pages of your book. And thank you, Stephanie, for your poems, read with much joy. The light of The Inner Temple will touch many hearts.

Ylana Hayward
(Leader of The White Eagle Lodge)

INTRODUCTION

This collection of meditations has grown out of genuine need of readers to understand the whole process of meditation more fully. By this I am not merely referring to the achievement of good practice, which is ongoing, but to the questions that can arise throughout regular practice. As, in essence, meditation is an alchemical process, transmuting the somewhat raw composition of the personality into a vessel worthy of bearing spiritual truth and wisdom, we cannot expect not to change. Quite naturally, with this change new insights emerge. Because the inner and outer experiences we may have throughout our meditational practise are somewhat personal, we may think we are alone in them and come to doubt their validity. Through the lens of *The Inner Temple,* Hanne sensitively addresses the questions, doubts and confusion that may sometimes arise in the meditation process. Always in matters of truth, nothing speaks louder than personal experience and throughout the twenty years Hanne has been practising meditation and holding groups within her own home, her insights have been many. She discusses the sort of feelings and thoughts which can come up throughout practice with empathy and clarity, yet also providing practical ways of dealing with these states of mind. Sensitively, yet with humour, she discusses the various games and skilful tricks our ego can play with us on the road to spiritual enlightenment.

Many of the meditations have appeared in the **Science of Thought Review* over the four years when Hanne ran the 'Meditation of the Month' series where readers often requested that she addresses a particular subject. Since then, Hanne has added chapters on Crystals, Colour and Essential Oils together with their use in meditation. Her former work as an aromatherapist has obviously broadened her insight into people's needs, as her training in teaching and counselling have made her practise very accessible to the reader.

There are many books on meditation today, quite rightly so, since it addresses a tremendous need in our Western culture to become more environmentally responsible and integrated caretakers of our fragile planet. There are diverse academic, devotional, esoteric, occult and practical meditational techniques available today which, en masse, can seem confusing and difficult to choose from. The quality which sets Hanne's meditations apart from many is their ability to combine the practical with the beautiful and spiritual. Their direct simplicity appeal to the mind and heart. In particular I enjoyed **Meeting with an Initiate**, where Hanne delightfully describes her meeting with the Dalai Lama when he visited Oslo. Here the humility she often discusses, comes to light through the medium of this very enlightened man.

Having worked very closely with Hanne over the past five years I have learned that she actually lives her meditations. And I can quite honestly say that she is one of the few people I have met who actually enjoys setting aside time for meditation daily. Unlike the rest of us, who battle a lot with self discipline and often with great reluctance apportion time to meditation, Hanne actually thrives on it! Over the years, she has helped me to see meditation not so much as a discipline, but both a necessity and a joyful exercise. I think this is one of the qualities that comes through in the book; the spontaneous joy that arises in her meditations and which, little by little, steals into the heart of the reader.

Stephanie Sorréll (Editor, **Science of Thought Review***)*

CHAPTER ONE
THE INNER LIGHT

*"Let your spirit so shine before men
that they may see their Christ in you."*

White Eagle

In Norway, where I grew up, the official state religion is Lutheran Protestantism. My parents, however, were not what you might call religious people, so religion was rarely mentioned in our home. When I was a child and asked if my mother believed in God, she replied by saying that she believed in all that is good and that to her was God. This answer she gave after careful consideration. However, the official Lutheran teaching believes that all people are sinners by birth and that the only way to obtain salvation is through the recognition that Jesus, the man, is the (only) Son of God and to confess this belief verbally. This is the only way to salvation and eternal life.

The only so-called Christian person in my family was my mother's aunt, who expressed concern that I did not attend Sunday School, so my mother consented to my aunt to take me to their church Sunday School. This was my first encounter with the above doctrine. I will never forget my reaction (I was only five or six years old at the time). The Sunday School teacher told us, with tears running down her cheeks, how sad it was that all those children in Africa and other remote places on our Earth had to go to Hell because no one had told them about Jesus. I was absolutely shocked! That surely was not these childrens' fault! However, children can be very logical and I gave it a couple of days' thought and came to the conclusion that if there was a God at all whatever he might be, he certainly would not be unfair! So I approached my mother and declared that I did not think she should let me go back to Sunday School any more, because they were lying there. (These words have later been related back to me.) My mother, in her wisdom, did not send me back to Sunday School.

I do not think I thought much about religion after that. That was it! However, deep down I must have known that if a

God existed it was a God of unconditional love and justice, and which I can remember feverishly arguing for during our religious classes at school. It was not until I reached my early twenties that a spiritual stirring of the heart sent me into a series of events and soul searching which brought me to the quote at the beginning of this article. The moment I "quite by chance" opened a book and saw those words I thought: "Yes, that is it, this is what I believe."

That was when my conscious inner journey began, after which it has been a life long quest towards developing the Christ within so that my light may grow to reach the lives of others – human, animal and nature. It is also a truth that I have found to be at the heart of all religions and mystical teachings. Although that "light" is called by different names. And one of the methods to develop and become conscious of this inner light is through meditation.

YOUR TRUE SELF, AND THE PURPOSE OF MEDITATION

If people ask me why I meditate, I usually give the answer: "To become more fully myself."

On more than one occasion this has brought a look of either confusion or disapproval in people's eyes, if not expressed verbally. I admit that I give this answer to be a bit provocative, and to remind myself and others about who and what we are: We are spiritual beings having an earthly experience, and not the other way around. So when I say I meditate in order to become more myself, I am not of course referring to the little self, the personality, but the Greater Self which is of the spirit and one with God – the Christ Self. The more often we can be in contact with and conscious of this Greater Self, the more of this can permeate our daily life, and the easier it is to keep this line of contact in the turmoil of earthly life so that it can constantly work through the personality and guide our thoughts and actions. As Mr Hamblin says: "The Christ Child within grows and expands until He takes entire charge of our life; then the old self is obliterated and we know it no more."

So to me, meditation is like a journey into that Self – the I AM which the mystics of all time have known and which Jesus talked about when he said: "I AM the Light of the World. I AM the Way, the Truth and the Life." The I AM which is the Christ in every man, woman and child.

When we meditate all the things we do have the purpose of leading us into that point of our total being. I find it helpful to think of it as the layers of an onion. The first layer is the physical body, and our first task is to make sure that this body is comfortable and relaxed so that it does not interfere with our journey inwards. (It is amazing how much little aches and itches can draw our attention away.) Next, we need to still the mental clutter and activity in the mental body. To do this, we use our breathing technique and choose an image we can focus the mind upon. In the West the mind is so strong that making it blank is almost impossible. By doing this we will find that the next layer starts to calm down too – the emotions, which are like a sea that needs to become perfectly still so that it can reflect the perfect image of the Greater Self rather than the distorted reflections you get when the surface is broken by movement. It is at this point that we enter into the higher consciousness using our higher emotional and higher mental bodies which are part of our Eternal

Self. And from here our Greater Self will lead us to the I AM – the flame in the Temple of our Spirit.

Creative meditation is one of many methods. But it is a safe method, because you are in control, and you are using your own tools which are your senses. All our physical senses have a spiritual counterpart which we use in creative meditation.

And when we have experienced the I AM, we know that all life is ONE. We know that God is all LOVE, we know that we are not separate from God or our brother/sister or any part of God's Creation. We know the truth of Jesus' words about what we do to others we do to him, we do to ourselves. Only in consciousness are we separate from God and His creation be it human, animal, plant or mineral – even angels…

CHAPTER TWO

PREPARING YOURSELF FOR MEDITATION

"If we train the mind to become still a few minutes every day, and filled with a restful thought or idea of Divine Truth, a feeling of renewed life and inspiration takes possession of us."

Henry Thomas Hamblin

Here are a few hints that may be helpful in your meditation:

1. Find yourself a peaceful corner where you know you will not be disturbed.

2. If possible try to keep your time of meditation as regular as possible. It is so easy for the lower mind to find excuses for not doing it if you try to fit it in at your convenience.

3. It is also very helpful to have a beautiful, but simple physical focal point for your meditation such as a candle, a beautiful flower or a picture of your Master. After a while, you will find that a lovely peaceful atmosphere is being created here which will help you in your meditation.

4. Many people also find that starting their quiet time with a piece of music helps them to still their being.

5. When you feel comfortable and at peace, you can start your meditation. Breathe a little deeper while listening to your breath for a little while. This will help you to still the busy daily mind. Then gradually concentrate your whole being upon God – upon Good which is the Light, and that Light shines within us all… Feel God's love and light pour into you as you breathe in the Breath of God – as if the very light from the sun or a star is shining into your heart…

If during this exercise you should find your mind starts to wander (which it most likely will), do not worry – just observe your thoughts and let them go, then – start again. Do not give up, but keep on trying in a relaxed manner.

Many people find it very helpful to meditate in a group, not only because of the support of the build up of energy which makes it easier to stay focused, but also because they find that by listening to another person they do not have to open their eyes to look at the text or worry about whether they remember.

If you do not have access to a group, the next best thing you can do is to read the meditation text onto a cassette yourself. Make sure you read it in your 'best' possible voice slowly and with the appropriate pauses for quiet and meditation. Maybe you also have a friend who can share your meditation with you. I have had many people say how helpful they have found this.

Whether you use a tape recorder or not, do not forget to first relax your body and still your mind by using your breathing before starting your visualisation exercise. As Hamblin says: "There is a breathing of the spirit, just as there is a breathing of the physical lungs. In the same way that this outward body breathes air, so is it possible for the awakened soul to breathe the finer ethers of the breath of God."

CLOSING RITUAL
A FEW WORDS ABOUT ENDING YOUR MEDITATIONS

The Tree Blessing

*May you be like a tree whose roots
quarry deep into the earth's wisdom.
So that your mind is filled with vision and inspiration.
May you grow strong like a tree knowing
your growth, however slow and painful,
is not just for yourself
But for this lovely planet.
May you pause like the tree to feel
the gentle winds of heaven upon you.
And the heart of the Creator warm and golden within you.
May you be wise as the tree who taps
the centre of its being for truth.
So that amidst every storm that shakes
your roots you will know that all is well.
Within your still centre may you know
the magic of love that opens all doors
and heals all pain.*

*May you always be strong and firm
and beautiful as a tree...*

Stephanie Sorréll

An equally important part of your meditation to that of the opening ritual is the closing ritual. This is especially so if you have been in a very deep meditation or feel you have been 'away' for a long time. To make full use of our times of quiet we need to be fully awake and aware on a physical level. We are of no use to ourselves or others if we float about in a dreamlike haze throughout the day. We will soon feel depleted and out of focus, and we would be like a leaf in the wind rather than a tree with its roots deeply buried in Mother Earth, strong enough to cope with the storms of life without losing our centre and our ground.

If we have only been meditating very lightly it is enough to just gently regain our focus and with a few deep breaths make a conscious link with the body and the ground below us, feeling that we are firmly rooted like the tree in our bodies and in Mother Earth. Then see yourself in a cross of light encircled by God's protective light around you. I also usually see myself enveloped in a cloak of light.

If you have been going deeper into meditation, there might be a need to close down the windows of your soul or the so-called psychic centres in your soul body – sometimes called chakras. These are centres in our light body, seen clairvoyantly as swirling vortexes of energy in our etheric or light body. These vortexes are connected to the major endocrine glands in the physical body, and are situated at the base of the spine (the base chakra), the spleen chakra which is situated at the back on the left hand side below the shoulder blade. (Some schools of teaching follow the Eastern tradition that the hara centre is used as the second chakra. This is situated below the navel. According to teachers like White Eagle the spleen is used to reach the hara. This seems to be a method better suited to our Western bodies.) The third centre is the solar plexus, situated just above the navel. The heart centre is placed in the middle of the chest (not to the left like the physical heart), rather slightly above, and right in the middle. Then there is the throat centre which is at the base of the throat or neck. The brow centre is in the middle of the brow as the name indicates, and finally the crown at the top of the head. All these chakras are connected with certain spiritual and psychic functions and colours, but this is beyond the scope of this book.

When you are in deep meditation these centres are activated and become more open and need to be closed down afterwards. There are many ways of doing this. I will offer two methods here, and you will have to decide which one suits your need at any time.

A: When you have gone through a gradual returning to your physical consciousness, (and do take your time with this process) and you feel perfectly grounded and centred, see your chakras in the following manner. On each centre – one at a time starting with the crown – you see a white open lotus, then see this lotus closing up like the lotus does at night. Then seal it with an equal sided cross of light encircled by light. (This is a very powerful symbol and as old as the history of humankind.) Then go to the next chakra, the brow and do exactly the same, then the throat, heart, solar plexus, spleen (or hara) and the base of spine. Then end the way I described earlier in the simple closing ritual.

B: The following closing ritual is the most protective and complete closing ritual I know, and is thought so by the White Eagle Lodge. You follow the same procedure as above, but instead of using the symbol of the lotus just seal each of the seven chakras with the cross of light encircled by light. Then using your breath as you inhale, draw a circle of light starting from the ground by your left foot, and imagine this light passing through your foot and up the left side of your body to the crown. Then on the outbreath you see the circle of light pass through the right side of your body till the circle is complete, meeting under your feet. Do this seven times. This is called "the seven fold breath". Really feel yourself encircled by this protective light as you do it.

The next step is called the "spiral of light". In one breath encircle you body in a spiral of light, clockwise. See the spiral starting from the ground by your feet and encircling your body in seven spiralling rings and finishing at the crown. Then on the outbreath imagine the light going straight into the ground like a rod of light really grounding you. You are now well protected and ready to re-enter the everyday world.

Finally a very common question. "If I close my chakras, does that mean that I shut out all the good and light energies as well as the negative ones? My answer is definitely NO! I find it very sad when I hear people saying: "Oh no – I don't want to close myself down because I don't want to shut my guide out, or the spiritual energies around me." And they wonder why they feel depleted and find it difficult to function in a hard world because they are so sensitive ! The true spiritual energies are not blocked out. This is simply not how we are made. You can compare it to a fishing net. The width of the mesh in the net decides what size fish you will catch. High spiritual energies swing very fast and on a graph would show as very small lines. While negative coarse energies would show up as tall and wide and slow. The veil protecting our psychic centres is made to let these small fast ones in. But if you open the door you will be open to all kinds of "fish", so when you seal your centres you simply make sure that your door is closed so that only that which is meant to enter will enter. And believe me, you will not advance spiritually by escaping the world and living your life in a semi-physical dreamworld which you might think at the time is very spiritual. Remember you are responsible for your own life, so be like the tree not like the falling leaf.

INNER FLAME MEDITATION

Now quietly and gently prepare yourself for your time of inner communion. When your body feels relaxed and comfortable, start your breathing exercise and gradually use your breathing to consciously breathe in the light from the shining star above you (symbol of the higher self) until your whole being is vibrating with light. You now realise that you are standing on the shore of a peaceful lake. The surface is silvery, yet containing all the colours of the rainbow when the sun's rays are playing upon it. Feel the quiet movement of the water against your feet as you let your breath follow the gentle rocking of the water against your feet....

In this state of calm and peace visualise a pure white flame burning in your heart. It is so still – and warm. And it is almost as if it is resting upon the water. Then again be aware of the sun/star shining above you and into you reaching and nourishing the flame within, and as it does so the flame grows in brilliance and strength until the flame and the sun/star become one light.

You are light.. And you remember the words of Jesus: "I AM the resurrection and the life." The I AM, the real you is the resurrection and the life. The Christ – in you. This is the door to the Kingdom. Take the Master's hand and follow him……

Pause

When you are ready prepare yourself to gently come back in consciousness to your everyday life, but before you do "we give as we have received" and just very gently let the light and love and peace go from your heart to any person or area in life that you feel are in need of this – just for a few moments without emotional and mental strain. Then firmly bring yourself back. Be aware of your body, the room around you etc. Feet on earth, head in the sun. Then see yourself as a cross of light in a protective circle of light (feeling your feet growing roots into the earth if you still feel a bit ungrounded). Then go upon your way with a thankful heart. *

MUSIC AND INSPIRATIONAL WRITINGS AS TOOLS IN MEDITATION

I mentioned earlier that it is helpful to start your quiet time by listening to a piece of beautiful music. Some pieces of classical music that I find helpful for this purpose are: J.S Bach's *Air*, Faure's *In Paradisum*, Lloyd-Webber's *Pie Jesu*, Albinoni's *Adagio*, Barber's *Adagio*. If you are more into New Age music there is a lot to choose from on the market. However, personally I prefer the classical for their greater variety and sound. You can also instead or in addition to the music read a piece of

---

* or any of the alternative closing rituals according to your need.

inspirational writing – preferably from a source with which you feel in tune. An excellent book of Mr Hamblin's for this purpose is "GOD OUR CENTRE AND SOURCE". Another book I would also recommend is "MEDITATION" by Grace Cooke as, in addition to lovely pieces for readings, it also contains valuable information on meditation in the Western mystical tradition.

An example of such is from "GOD OUR CENTRE AND SOURCE" and is called *God, the Giver of Life.*

"If we wait upon the Lord, looking ever deeper and deeper within our own soul, we come at last to the One Life which is our true centre, and with which we are one for ever.

In this One Life we are one with every living creature. In fact, in our highest moments of realisation it seems as though, in our most interior selves, we are the life which animates all living creatures. We experience a lovely and delicious unity with all creation – the rising of the sun, and the going down of the sun: the birds and animals and other creatures: the flowing and ebbing of tides, the stars coming nightly to the sky.

But this, after all, in spite of being so interior, is only the shell of the great mystery. We go still deeper, and find ourselves truly one with the One Source of all. We enter into timelessness; we are in the eternal Now. We find ourselves one with That which changes not; we realise that we are established in the Eternal, and that our true life is lived in God."

A SPRING MEDITATION

Again we start our meditation by spending a few moments concentrating on our breathing – and as we aspire towards God we gradually quite consciously breathe in the Light of God, gently and peacefully until we feel filled with light and are centred under the ray of light from the Source of Being. When we are filled with light, we also become aware that the separation between us and other life forms and other people starts to dissolve. This is because we start to identify not so much with our personality as with our spiritual self and in the spiritual world (which is also on earth) there is no separation.

We now visualise that we are entering a beautiful sunlit garden full of young life. We feel the anticipation before the breaking forth of the new life of spring. You are not alone in this garden. Friends of your spirit are with you, and also those of the animal kingdom who are also waiting for spring to bloom. If you are very still you can almost hear the buds popping open. And the birds join in with their song of praise to the Creator and His Creation.

You become drawn to a part of the garden where the golden flowers – the daffodils – grow. You watch a young golden bud opening up under the ray of the sun. You meditate here feeling your heart opening and expanding as you are drawn right into the heart of this golden flower – your own golden heart…

Gradually you become aware of the form of a human figure in the centre of this golden radiance. His heart and face shines like the sun, His arms outstretched to greet you. The Christ in human form. Surrender your soul to Him and receive His divine Love… In this union you truly understand the words "I and my Father are one"…

Pause

Before you return to your daily tasks, for a few moments join Him in His outpouring of Love and Life to those who suffer or are in need of help (people, animals or nature). Then, with thankfulness, use your breath to bring your consciousness right back to your daily life – firmly but gently.

You might choose to close your quiet time with a prayer. I will share with you one of my favourites. It is taken from the book; **Prayer in the New Age** *by White Eagle:*

"Great White Spirit of the open spaces, the mountain tops and the quiet peaceful valleys; Great White Spirit of nature and the heavens above the earth, and the waters beneath. Great White Spirit of eternity, infinity, we are enfolded within Thy great heart. We rest our heart upon Thy heart. Great Father and Mother God we love, we worship Thee; we resign all into Thy loving keeping knowing that Thou art love, and all moves forward into the Light."

Then see yourself strong in the cross of light encircled by light – feet on Mother Earth head in the Heavens, and the cloak of God around you.

CHAPTER THREE
THE FESTIVALS

OUR INNER CYCLES

I have often found that it is helpful to follow the seasons and the religious festivals in my meditations, as the collective and spiritual energy seems to be there supporting my own inner rhythms. These religious festivals are very much an outer expression of our inner life and the cycles of nature. They speak to us, not only of the journey of the soul towards Christedness or Union with the Divine, but also about the process of meditation. Before Christmas we have the period of advent – the waiting time – which can be compared with the time of preparation when we start our meditation – the stilling process. Then comes Christmas where we, like the shepherds and the Wise Men, follow the Star to find the Christ child – the Christ within – which rests in the humble cave/stable, the heart centre which can only be found if we are humble enough to recognise the true light of the spirit, not amidst the outer glory of mammon, materialism or mental pride. It is to follow the path of the heart-mind. Having found the Christ child within we carry it with us, but in order for it to grow we have to go through the winter process (the crucifixion) – a time when nature surrenders. I say *surrender* rather than die, because if you look at a tree, the new bud is already formed as the leaves fall off in the autumn. But nature surrenders itself and draws its life force inwards so that which has outgrown its function can give room for the new life. There is such peace in surrender. In my own country this is so obvious in winter. When nature has surrendered, it is covered by a beautiful white carpet of peace. This is the state of consciousness we need to attain in our meditation to receive and be able reflect this heavenly peace. I have often thought to myself when I have walked among this white beauty how impossible it would be for men to make war if they had seen and felt nature like this. So when our desires, our unruly emotions, our great mental activity have surrendered itself to the Divine Peace, the sun comes again and quickens all life into growth. The Christ child awakens to rise up to new life and can burst forth in all its glory to radiate our whole being (the resurrection), and our spirit can blossom like the flower and we experience the ultimate bliss.

If we can only hold this state of consciousness for a few seconds in our meditation, we will also have understood a little more of what is waiting for every child of God – a saint and master in the making. Our goal: the resurrected man/woman.

MEDITATION FOR SPRING

After you have gone through your process of preparation and become very still in mind, body and emotions, try to visualise that you are in a beautiful winter landscape. Use all your senses to breathe in the cool fresh air. Hear the song of the birds in early spring and see the sun playing upon the white snow crystals making the white carpet look as if it is covered in jewels reflecting all the colours of the rainbow. Then gradually you just feel how the sun is becoming warmer and brighter and you notice that the snow starts melting away. In its place you see the green shoots, the snowdrops, the daffodils and the crocuses pushing their way up through the earth. Just inhale the feeling of spring and let it flood your being and allow the song of spring to rejoice in your heart. Then for a moment you become aware of your angel's wings around you and together you become like one of those flowers, and you feel how your heart opens and your spirit is taken on angel's wings into the very heart of the sun and you are flooded by the Light of the Christ Sun – the Son of God.

Pause

When you feel ready you may want to share what you have received and send out from your heart to those in darkness or to those who suffer; and see the peace of humankind walking in brotherhood upon Mother Earth, radiating love from their hearts. Then give thanks from your heart to your Creator and bring yourself firmly into your everyday consciousness, feet on earth, head in the sun. *Then see yourself as a cross of light encircled in the protective circle of the love of God.*

Finally, I would like to share with you this quote from the book, ***The Way of the Sun*** by White Eagle:

> "The ancient festival of welcoming the sun at this season of the year will be revived when men realise the true art of life. The Sun of God (by which we mean the life-force which flows from the heart of God, which is love) will enter in fullness and richness into man's being in the same way as the sun enters into the seed quickened to life in Mother Earth. As nature is quickened by the same force of love, so man will be quickened and grow to perfection. There will be in those days not stricken men and women, but all will be as perfect sons of God."

A CHRISTMAS MEDITATION

At this time of the Christ-mass, let us be like the Wise Men of old who followed the Star. Use your creative imagination and see this beautiful Star, symbol of the higher self shining in the heaven. You walk its path of light until you feel quite centred under it, and it appears to stand quite still.

Visualise now a cave with a little light flickering inside. You enter the cave – the cave of your heart where the Christ light burns, and you see the little Christ babe lying in a manger – the simple, humble heart. It is surrounded by the Father (Power) and the Mother (Wisdom). Looking closer you will find that the manger is like the petal of a rose-symbolic of the love in your heart...

You see that the light in the cave is the light which is radiating from the Child in the manger. And in your soul you kneel and worship the Child. As you open your heart in worship, the light grows stronger and stronger – and gradually you become enveloped in its radiance... You become one with it – the Christ within you...

(From here you continue on your own)

When you feel ready and when your heart is filled with love, you give as you have received, and you think of any situation or person which is in need of help and enlightenment. And with the power of your soul send out love and light to them for a moment.

Now with deep thankfulness in your hearts, gradually bring yourself back into your daily consciousness. Again breathe slowly and deeply and make sure that you are perfectly centred, with feet firmly on Mother Earth before you continue your daily life. You might find it helpful to see yourself as an equal sided cross of light within a circle of light-perfectly balanced and with the protective cloak of Light around you.

Other seasonal meditations on page 26, 64 and 115

CHAPTER FOUR
FINDING A TEACHER AND FOLLOWING THE HEART

I read the following story in a book called "God Loves Laughter" by William Sears. Somehow its simple profound message has stayed with me ever since. I read it about 10 years ago. I believe it has a lesson to teach all students on the path. It is called THE LIGHT.

"Once upon a time there was a little boy. With all his family and friends he was lost in the valley of darkness. Then, quite by accident he found a flashlight. When he switched on the light of the torch everybody in the dark valley saw it and came hurrying towards it. With his light, the little boy began to lead the people out of the valley of darkness and up the path of the mountainside. First a

hundred followed him, then a thousand, then tens of thousands. Every time he looked back there were more people behind him. The more people he saw, the more pleased he became with himself and the fine work he was doing. He kept looking back more frequently to see how many he was leading out of the darkness. How proud he was that so many people were following him. But then he stumbled and dropped the torch which was scooped up by someone behind him. The crowd tramped over him and left him in the dust as they swept up the hill. They had not been following him at all. It was the light they were following, and without it he was left in the darkness."

For many of you the symbolism of the story will be familiar. The torch symbolises the inner Light; the dark valley, the materialistic consciousness and our lower nature; the mountain top, our higher consciousness to which we are aspiring.

To me the messages are many in this story. Firstly it is interesting that it is a child that carries the light. Did not Jesus ask us to become as little children again in order to enter the Kingdom of Heaven?

The fact that he *found* the torch suggests that the light does not belong to the personality who lives in the dark valley. And is it not a warning to us all on the path when people come to us for help, healing and counselling that we remember that it is not the personality we wear in incarnation that attracts people to us, but the light of God which shines in us? And may we pray that we will never forget this. Jesus himself said: "It is not me, but the Father in me that doeth the work." To me this suggests that it is our divine nature that can lead others *and* our own lower nature to "the mountain top", not the earthly personality.

The greatest stumbling block on the path of recognition is naturally pride and lack of humility which also lead to "the fall" of this boy. But it also applies to us all whatever our work or station in life.

This message has also something to teach to today's seekers on the path at a time where there is a guru and a teacher around every corner. Do they claim the glory for themselves, or do they recognise themselves as merely channels for the Divine? And we would be wise not to fall into the trap of personal worship of these teachers by putting them on a pedestal, depriving them of all their "humanity"– which, if they are true teachers, is the last thing they would want. No one is more humble and aware of their humanness than a true spiritual leader. Otherwise we may one day suffer great disappointment when we find out that they were only human after all. And our reaction may be one of aggression and rejection because they were not living up to the image we put upon them, which after all is not fair. Have they been tempted to want this worship? Well, that's another lesson.

Humility is such a misunderstood word. So often confused with cowardice or putting oneself down. But humility is knowing that you are neither better nor worse than anybody else in the sight of God. Or as my friend, Sister Helen says: "To know your own worth before God is true humility."

THE TEMPLE AT THE TOP OF THE MOUNTAIN

Now let us for our meditation pray to God that we may receive help to lay aside the outer personality of our daily life and enter into our place of silence. To still the outer mind remember to use your breath in this process, then see before you in the stillness of your heart a little flame burning – so pure and gentle. Gradually we become aware of it as our little lamp shining in the dark wood. An invisible hand lifts the lamp up and bids us to follow. (You can imagine it as the invisible hand of God, your Master, your higher self or your guardian angel – whatever feels helpful to you.) It leads you out of the dark wood until you come to a mountain. Here your inner eyes are beginning to open and you can see the mountain, and on the mountain top shines a brilliant light, like a sun or a star.

*You now stand at your chosen path that will take you to the mountain top, and you start the climbing, the ascent. Sometimes it is hard, other times easier, but as you keep your eyes on the light shining above you, you gradually become aware of the "Everlasting Arms" carrying you along, and sometimes a brother ahead of you on the path reaches down to help you over a difficult patch also. And more and more you feel the light drawing you and filling you as you move nearer to the light ... Until you reach the top and you find yourself before a beautiful shining temple – the temple of your Spirit. You enter the temple whose two entrance pillars are called Humility and Simplicity, and you worship at the altar here in the silence of the temple of your heart, which is where you will find your Master, the Christ within. Here you **know** that all is well, all is in the hands of the Divine. Rest your weary soul and receive the Divine Blessing from your Father-Mother God.*

PAUSE

When you feel ready you radiate from your heart a blessing to those who suffer and have their consciousness in the "dark wood" and see their lights start flickering. You do this without any sense of judgement. Just a gentle, loving radiation from the heart in blessing.

Then gradually start the descent down the mountain side into your everyday consciousness – bringing the light with you in your heart and mind.

Firmly and with thankfulness feel your feet on Mother Earth and God's protective cloak around you. See yourself as a cross of light encircled by light. Then go upon your way asking God to sustain your work and life.

MEETING WITH AN INITIATE

Only when trained and disciplined through contact with Divine Love does man's intellect change into divine intelligence. That is why all great souls become gentle and simple, sweet, childlike, and of goodly intelligence. The arisen Christ is born from the heart, not from the intellect.

White Eagle

It is very easy to be swept off one's feet by many of the charismatic teachers and leaders of religions and groups today. It is often difficult to know the wheat from the chaff. At the beginning of our conscious path of spiritual growth and unfoldment, it is natural to seek for an "ideal" or "Guiding Star" to follow. And there are many wonderful known and unknown "stars" out there during this time of great changes in the history of human evolution. The Mayan people speak of the time from 1997 to 2012 as "the time of awakening" when the ancient wisdom is going to be released to all peoples before the next world age begins after the present one ends in 2012. But where there is an increase of light there is bound to be an increase of the opposite, and we have to learn to discern.

I have found that the above quote of White Eagle's has helped me more than once when I have tried to navigate between the many teachers out there. Great charisma and a magnetic personality or high flying words are not necessarily identical to being a true light-bearer. One person always springs to mind as a great example of the above quote, and that is His Holiness the Dalai Lama of Tibet. I have been so fortunate as to be present at two of his lectures in Oslo, and on both occasions he passed me, almost touching my shoulder. One of the lectures was in connection with receiving the Nobel Peace Prize, the other one was a talk he gave called "A Human Approach to World Peace". I remember the essence of his message being that the only solution to all global problems lies in universal brotherhood, including brotherhood with the animals. He said that compassion and communication from the heart is fundamental for world peace. He expressed that every human being has a universal responsibility, no matter what religion, ideology or belief system; all have to come together on this common ground.

His wisdom may be obvious to all, and he is probably one of the best trained religious scholars in the world, but what comes across when you see and hear him is his absolute childlike spontaneity. In the middle of his lectures he can burst out in giggles (often to the embarrassment of his disciples). He is absolutely himself all the time. And he admits that he finds it hard to live up to serious occasions like at the Nobel Peace talk he gave. On the mentioned occasion he said he would try to behave as was expected of him, while stars of laughter beamed from his eyes, and you had a feeling that he thought it was quite unnecessary. He says: "I am just a simple Buddhist monk." Another seemingly striking contradiction in his nature was also apparent. You see this gentle, compassionate, childlike man sitting there, but as he walked passed me I felt an incredible power sweeping through me. The strength and the love that came from his aura completely opened my heart, and I knew I was in the presence of a great initiate. He seemed to have the same effect on the whole overcrowded university hall, whether people were conscious of it or not, judging from the awe that seemed to sweep through the audience as he walked down the aisle. I had not expected the intensity of his strength and power, and it proves to me what real strength is, which reminds me of the little mushroom pushing through the tarmac. The legendary American Indian King Eagle is famous for his words:

*"Nothing is as strong as gentleness,
and nothing is as gentle as real strength."*

Something else we can learn from this is to let go of all pretence, trying to look or sound important. In so-called spiritual circles you so often see people with either a sanctimonious or a "holier than Thou" look about them. It is this "trying to be something that we are not" which becomes such a barrier between people and is a great hindrance to true communication. Jesus himself taught us that unless we become as children, we will not enter the Kingdom of Heaven.

True wisdom is to let the heart illumine the mind. The mind can be arrogant and the slayer of the real, but the heart, when it is open, is childlike, simple and loving. And many of the tests we go through on the spiritual path is to see whether we are true to our inner light which dwells in our heart, in other words if we have the strength and the courage to follow our hearts. White Eagle says to his students (from **The Quiet Mind**):

"Be true. This is the essence of the spiritual life. The note of the spirit is sounded on the higher planes, and the knocks you receive in everyday life are to test you, whether you can ring true. To ring true you must always sound the note of God, or good, which is within you."

And as we learn to depend on our own guiding light, we find that our Master and Teacher has been there all along within us – within our own heart.

THE JEWEL IN THE HEART

When you are comfortable and relaxed in body, and you have stilled your mind and emotions, be aware of your breathing. Gently observe it becoming slightly deeper, until it has found its own gentle rhythm. Aspire to the highest you know and open yourself to the brilliant light shining down upon you, and you breathe it in until it fills your whole being.

You become aware of having been raised in consciousness and gradually you notice a dazzling light shining in front of you. It is like a big diamond reflecting all the colours of the rainbow. The light is pure and gentle, in fact the stronger the light grows the more you become aware of the supreme gentleness of the love that is enfolding you and filling you. Until your heart cannot help but open wide to this beautiful Divine Love.

As you surrender to this love, you lift your gaze and you look into a pair of eyes that are full of love and compassion (but also notice the twinkle in the eyes). And you realise that the jewel you have seen and felt is the heart of your Master... Stay with your Master in communion heart to heart. In love there is no separation, and you can find him always – right there in your own heart.

PAUSE

Before you withdraw, send out this love and light which you have received to anyone you know is in need – without judgement or desire. Then gently withdraw in consciousness back to your everyday life. Use your breathing to bring yourself back firmly but gently. With thankfulness and joy in your heart, feel yourself properly grounded with feet on earth and head in heaven, see yourself in the centre of a cross of light encircled by light. Take the time you need in this process.

PATH OF THE HEART

Today seekers on the path towards enlightenment are offered numerous spiritual methods and practises from many different gurus and teachers from all over the world. It can often be hard to make a choice, and we may be tempted to try a little bit of this and a little bit of that. But although it is necessary to realise that these methods in themselves may be good and true, it is important that we find a method which rings true to us, and which we feel comfortable and in harmony with. Maybe the reason why there are so many methods lies in the fact that we, at this stage of our evolution, have different needs. Take for example the ancient Eastern method of meditation of using a mantra (a syllable sounded repeatedly aloud or inside you). This is a very powerful method which can open the doors to depths inside us which, unless we are under a wise and strong teacher, can be too much for us to handle on our own. I have come across many cases of this, and have personal experience of it too. In our Western world today we have a complex nature, often with much emotional wounding which needs working on. Opening the doors to the subconscious too quickly can become a very unpleasant experience.

As a race we, in the West, are working to develop our minds which can at times be quite difficult to control. That is why for many of us the method of creative visualisation is a safe method of meditation. By creating beautiful images we have a method of focusing the mind. At the same time these beautiful and positive images stir our higher emotions towards love and peace.

The images we choose are of course essential, and Mr Hamblin always says that. "LOVE IS THE KEY". His contemporary mystic, Grace Cooke, says: "Throughout the ages philosophers, saints and sages, prophets, saviours and teachers have offered their followers a key which will unlock the door of heaven. THE KEY LIES WITHIN THE HEART; AND IT IS LOVE." That is why it is important that we concentrate our whole being upon God/Good when we start our meditation; for it is a journey towards the centre of our heart where the Christ Spirit dwells, the light of God which is in every man, woman and child. And the whole purpose of our meditation practice is to awaken and strengthen this aspect of our being, so that it can gradually rule more and more of our daily life and thinking – until we reach enlightenment or Christ consciousness. Again I quote from Grace Cooke's book, *Meditation*: "The goal of meditation is to bring all animal instincts of man under the control and direction of the Christ within the heart and so to achieve at-one-ment or union with God. This means that man, the microcosm, becomes consciously enfolded in the life of God, the macrocosm, the infinitely great."

And, please remember the goal, and do not think that it is the seeing of images and psychic impressions that is important. The images are just the *tools* towards finding the place of STILLNESS and peace within.

THE JEWEL IN THE LOTUS

To start your meditation you follow your usual ritual of relaxing music/prayer or whatever way you choose to still your being. Then concentrate your whole being upon God while you breathe a little more deeply and slowly (without straining). Gradually you become aware of the beautiful light from a sun or star shining down upon you, and you breathe in its light until it fills you completely.

Now visualise yourself in the perfect garden in a world which is full of light and beauty. Use your vision to create your own heavenly garden... In this garden you also see a circular pond. Together with your guardian angel you sit by the water to watch an exquisite white lily resting on its surface. Observe how the white petals unfold beneath the rays from the sun and see its golden heart being revealed. Feel the white and gold light radiating from it... and there in the centre rests the perfect jewel. "Behold the Jewel in the Lotus." And you let yourself become one with the lotus until the petals become the walls of your own inner temple, and its heart the golden altar within.

Worship here in the centre of your heart – in your own heavenly temple which is inside you and find union with God. "The Father and I are one."

PAUSE

When you feel ready and before you return to your everyday consciousness, radiate from your heart the Light and Love of God to any condition or person in need. Then bring yourself firmly back (connecting with the room around you) knowing that by having identified yourself with this ancient symbol of purity and truth you have received some of these qualities in your soul. See yourself in the cross of light encircled by light and the cloak of protection around you. Then with a thankful heart go upon your way of service – feet on Mother Earth, head in Heaven."

THE ROSE GARDEN

Just for a few moments concentrate on your breath. Listen to it and then gradually, while you are concentrating your whole being upon God and God's light, you breathe in His light as if the very Sun is pouring its rays upon you – until you feel filled with light. And if you have an area of your body which is aching or feels uncomfortable, direct extra light to this area. It is amazing how it works! The wonderful thing about our inner world is that although we might find the wintry months depressing and dark – we can always contact this inner universe for warmth, comfort and light.

Now visualise that you are standing in front of a lovely white gate which leads to a beautiful walled garden. Gently open the gate and enter. It feels warm and safe here... You feel the green grass underneath your feet as you walk along, and feel the support of the earth – the Earth Mother. The wind is gently caressing your cheek and playing in your hair. And you hear it singing in the trees along with the song of the birds in the garden... and you come to a little brook with crystal clear water. Feel its cleansing healing qualities as you bathe your feet in it and drink its water – while you watch the sun making millions of stars on the water when its rays hit the surface of the water – the water of your soul.

You now become aware of a wonderful scent of roses, and find yourself in a most exquisite rose garden. Just inhale the fragrance of these flowers, so often used as a symbol of love. And your attention is being led to one particular rose – a pink rose. See it opening its petals under the sun – revealing its golden heart in the centre. Breathe in its fragrance until you feel yourself enfolded in its petals – becoming one with it. It is as if you have entered the heart of the Divine Mother (which is also in you) whose symbol is the pink rose. Just rest here and know that all is well – all is taken care of – all is in God, the Divine Father-Mother's loving care. Just be and know that I AM God.

PAUSE

When you feel ready you can gradually breathe your way back into physical consciousness (which you have never really lost!!). Feet firmly on the ground as you feel yourself strongly connected with your physical body. Wrap your cloak of light around you and again see yourself as an equal sided cross within a circle of light - your roots growing from your feet into the earth. Then go upon your way in thankfulness for what you have received, bringing this light and love of God into your practical everyday life.

CHAPTER FIVE
CONTROLLING OUR EMOTIONS

I have, earlier in this book, written briefly about how important the breath is in order to control our unruly thoughts in meditation, combined with going back to our focal image. This does not mean feverishly trying to repress them, but rather just gently observe them, then let them go and return to your image. With patient and continuous practise this will almost become second nature to you.

But what about unruly emotions? You have probably all experienced how difficult it is to meditate under such conditions. And if we are deeply upset it might even sometimes be advisable just to try to calm down a bit and not attempt to go into deep meditation. Calming and stilling yourself could initially be attempted by listening to some soft relaxing music, reading some inspirational teaching or just simply concentrating on your breathing for a while and gradually imagining God's light and peace shining down upon you and into you. (Which it of course does all the time – it is only we ourselves who cut ourselves off from this Source of our being.)

We are all likely to have to deal with our emotions coming up when we meditate, and what can we do? Mr Hamblin says in his book, *His Wisdom Guiding:* "The more we fight our negative experiences the worse they appear, and the more completely defeated we become. This is because we are trying to fight evil on its own plane where it is all powerful. But, when we raise our consciousness to a higher level, we raise our problem or trouble to that plane where it never happened, and where evil has no power… Instead of fighting and resisting, we raise the whole trouble to that plane where harmony and order reign, and disharmony and disorder are, of course, quite unknown."

We are not here speaking of evil as such, but of negative emotions. Negative emotions cannot be solved on the plane of negative emotions. But as our feelings are so active at this point, it is better to work with them than to repress them. I find it helpful to use symbols that represent my emotions and feelings in this situation. And by using them in a positive way, raise them to a higher level. The most powerful symbol for the emotions and feelings is, of course, water. We speak often of the water of the soul, don't we? Time and time again I have found connecting with the water element so healing if I am emotionally troubled. Henry Thomas Hamblin uses the following imagery in *His Wisdom Guiding* which to me speaks so much about the feminine aspect of God, or God the Mother, if you like. That all embracing receptive embrace of the Divine Mother: "We are immersed in God, as a fish is immersed in water. Just as water is the natural element of a fish so also is God, the omnipresent Spirit, the natural element for us. We literally live, move and have our being in the One Spirit of Infinite Life. Its invisible rays of potent life pass into us and through us, and we are one with it.

At the same time we can rest in the Love of God, lean back on the Everlasting Arms and be at peace."

So let us use the symbol of the water for our meditation:

THE MASTER STILLING THE WAVES

Picture yourself standing barefooted by the shore of a beautiful lake or sea, and just for a moment feel the waves beating against your feet. Gradually you will find your breath adjusting to the movement of the water as you become attuned to it. You breathe in as the water rushes towards you and breathe out as the waves fall back. As you concentrate on this, your thoughts and feelings will gradually calm down and the waves transformed to the gentle rocking rhythm of the sea. Feel the peace of this gentle rocking movement and all your cares will leave you. And you might even feel the comforting wings of your angel around you. Your angel who is God's messenger to you and who will never leave you. Slowly you lift your gaze to the horizon and you see the rising sun casting a path of light across the water to you. In the centre of the sun you become aware of the form of the Great Master. He holds out His arms to welcome you. And you walk on the Path of Light across the water towards Him. (Some of you might, even as I do, prefer to stay in the water and just float or swim towards Him). Take as long as you need. Just concentrate your vision on that radiant, yet gentle form: all love, all light – no condemnation or judgement. And as you open your heart towards Him you will find that he comes towards you until you are caught up in His radiance and you become one with Him – if you will let yourself surrender to that Universal – yet very human LOVE. In that union you will find true PEACE – the peace of Heaven.

PAUSE

When you feel ready you might like to join all the others who meditate with you around the planet (for in spirit there is no time or space) to send this peace to the world as a gentle radiation from the heart.

You might like to end your meditation by sharing a prayer of Mr Hamblin's with me:

'Give thanks, O my soul, that there is nothing but God (good), and that God is infinite Love.

Give thanks that there is no disharmony in the Divine Mind, but only perfect harmony and peace.

Give thanks that there is no darkness, but only Light of Light."

Bring yourself firmly back into your daily life consciousness, feet on earth, head in Heaven. See yourself as a cross of light encircled by light as protection.

PRACTICAL THOUGHT CONTROL IN OVERCOMING DISTRACTIONS

"True Silence has a healing and restoring virtue. When we enter the true Silence we make it possible for a Divine adjustment to take place. The discordant, ill-balanced elements of our life become adjusted, and we enter into God's order and peace. We are led to make right decisions and to do just the right thing at the right time, and this makes for harmonious happenings in the outward life."

Henry Thomas Hamblin

I know that for many, finding silence or quietness can be the greatest obstacle to our daily meditations. Especially those who live in big cities, noise is a constant part of life. For others it can be children, relatives, neighbours etc. And often our mind tells us that we cannot meditate in this noise, and we are usually tempted to grab this excuse that the lower mind imposes upon us. However, Mr Hamblin says that "True Silence is not merely an absence of noise, but a state of consciousness which is above noise… this is not accomplished through the intellect, but through the heart." So what he is saying is that true Silence is a state of consciousness and has nothing to do with earthly noise.

So we can actually experience silence in the midst of noise. How can we do this? First it is important to understand that we must not fight or resist noise. Mr Hamblin says that it can only come through acceptance and co-operation. To illustrate this I will give an example. Two Fridays a year my landlady in the flat above mine in Norway had a women's party. This usually corresponded with our Friday meditation group. Our first reaction was: Oh no! But then we found that if we used the laughter and the fun upstairs to bring forth our own joy and blessed this moment of friendship and happiness in their lives, we soon found that if we could just leave them to it, so to speak, realising that we were in our own sacred space which nothing could penetrate – if we did not let it. As soon as we reached that realisation we found that they often moved to another part of the house where we could not hear them – or it ceased to bother us.

These things are often there for a purpose and give us an opportunity to control our minds. A practical exercise I find helpful is to imagine myself in a sound proof glass ball – knowing that nothing can actually penetrate this space, and what is outside has nothing to do with me then. I know this is not easy, but try… the reward is healing and a harmonious life as Mr Hamblin says above.

THE DOVE OF PEACE

Now before we start our meditation exercise, which is really just a tool to reach that place of true silence, make sure that you are comfortable – spine straight, shoulders relaxed, breathing a bit deeper and slower, concentrating your whole being upon God and God's Light. Consciously breathe in this light while you listen to your breath – no other sound exists. Do this until you feel still and filled with light. And know that you are not alone. In love, which is light, there is no separation between you and those you love, "here or there".

Gradually you imagine yourself sitting not in your chair, but in a lotus position (or on a white bench) in a beautiful sunlit garden. Before you is the surface of a still lake. You hear the rhythmic, gentle sound of water meeting the shore and gliding out again. And you will find that it has the same rhythm as your breathing. All cares and worries melt away in this place of peace and stillness. You see the light from the sun dancing stars on the water, while the song of the birds reaches your ears. And there, suddenly a white bird descends and settles in your hands – a dove. Feel its softness, its peace, its gentle love. You become so absorbed in this that you realise it is actually sitting in your heart. And gradually you become this dove (or if you cannot do this imagine yourself sitting on its back) and you feel yourself stretching your wings out as you fly up into the heart of the sun. (Birds are usually symbols for thought, and the dove, of course, is also symbol of the Spirit and of peace.)

Here in this state of higher consciousness you meditate in the Silence, God's Silence, and just let its infinite, blissful peace flow through you like a river …

"It is then that we realise that our life is as deep as the universe, and that it has infinite extensions beyond time and space, and that its roots are in God."

(H. T. Hamblin)

PAUSE

When you are ready, before you leave this state of consciousness, just for a moment radiate from your heart (not the mind) this feeling of peace and light to any dark area in the world (of your choice) and see it reaching the heart of the people there to bless and to heal, and ask that God may bless your work. Then bring yourself firmly back into your everyday consciousness. Feet with roots in Mother Earth and head in Heaven. Feel God's protective cloak become folded around you as you stand inside the circle of light as a cross of light, perfectly centred and grounded.

OVERCOMING FEAR AND UNWANTED THOUGHTS

"One of the lessons which the candidate on the path to spiritual illumination has to learn is that nothing can really touch or hurt him... No harm can touch the real you. Encourage this thought until it is always with you. Nothing can harm you and there is nothing to fear except fear."

White Eagle

There is nothing to fear except fear – a very powerful statement. It actually says that without fear *all* is well. I read a book recently called *Emissary of Light* by James F. Twyman. This book is based on the same theme and also explains the root of our fear:

"The first fearful, untrue and illusory thought on which every other thought is based is simply this: You are separate from God. In perceiving yourself as separate from God you have created a world where you are separate from and threatened by everything. And yet if the foundation of fear is false, then so is each thought that has come from that foundation. Take away this belief and everything above crumbles. Every building has a cornerstone. If the cornerstone is moved then the building cannot support itself. There is no need to release all the surrounding blocks of fearful beliefs you have. Simply release the idea that you are separate from God and the dream of separation ends on its own."

So what this is saying is that all hate, intolerance, judgement, cruelty, abuse etc. in the world is rooted in this one fundamental untruth – our belief that we are separate from God, or our *fear* that we are separate from God.

So how can we start to remove this cornerstone which we have built our lives, our society, our world upon? I believe that the more often we can experience being one with God and all life the less substance this cornerstone will have. This can sometimes be experienced in nature, through exquisite beauty and art, through complete union with another in a loving relationship, through the love of a child or an animal etc. In short, we gain this sense of unity through Love – because God is Love. But you are not dependant on anything or anyone outside yourself to experience this, because you are a spiritual being and the spirit of God or Love is in you. And right there in the centre of your heart you can experience that which is the goal of all mystics of the world: union with the Beloved. The most helpful way to find this is through daily prayer and meditation.

It is not only in our daily life we come across this cornerstone, but indeed also in our meditation. However, the good news is that it is during these moments that we can consciously recognise and work on this. Mr Hamblin and all true teachers remind us again and again of the importance of thought control and quieting our unruly emotions. (It is important here to remind ourselves that "control" does not mean "suppress".) James Twyman reminds us also that there is nothing "wrong" with our feelings, that they are just an energy. It is our judgement (which is a thought) of that feeling which decides how that feeling will be expressed. This judgement is rooted in fear. For instance if in your meditation you feel an upsurge of passionate feelings, your reaction might instinctively be one of fear and your mind immediately interferes and says: "No, you must not feel like this! Naughty!" Because maybe you have been brought up to think of passionate feelings as sinful and unwanted, in which case this feeling may express itself as confusion and anxiety and your meditation is ruined by guilt and depression – even self punishment. If you could instead make your mind step back and refrain from judgement, you could take hold of that energy and bring it up into your heart and send it out as light to the world, and it will be released for the good of all. Or if you are feeling resentful about something or someone which usually means that this person or situation in reality has made you feel fearful or threatened in some way and you have chosen to express it as resentment or judgement, do not judge yourself for feeling the way you do, or judge the feeling itself. Let go the mind and bring the feeling or energy up into your heart and send it out as light. White Eagle says in his book; *Spiritual unfoldment II:* "The solar fire, the creative fires which dwell in man can appear in frightening forms and threaten to overwhelm the life… Once controlled, it is raised into the heart as love and into the head as divine intelligence. When complete control is lacking it comes out in bad temper. But once this light, this life force rises into the heart, it manifests as great warmth of love, sweetness and sympathy."

If it is a thought that is getting in your way which is not accompanied by any particular feeling, like for instance tomorrow's shopping list or something very trivial, do not get caught up in it with your feelings by becoming annoyed or irritated with yourself. Merely stand back firmly centred in your heart and observe it – and you will gradually see it disintegrating by itself. It melts away because you have not given it any energy, you have not fed it. Then go back to the focus of your meditation.

(I just want to add here that there are times in our lives when our mental and emotional conflicts are so deep that it is advisable not to try to cope on our own like this, but rather to seek help from a professional person like a counsellor or spiritual teacher. It is not a sign of weakness or defeat to seek help if we get stuck on our own. On the contrary, we are all One and One in God and sometimes we need a little help from our extended Self in the guise of another person. This can be a both humbling experience and one of deep gratitude.)

MEDITATION ON THE GROWTH FROM A SEED

Now prepare yourself as usual and when you feel peaceful and absolutely comfortable, concentrate a while on your breathing and feel yourself being filled with God's light as you breathe in the light from the sun or star of your higher self, your source of light which is in the heart of God. Lift your heart to God in gratitude for all life and for all you have learned during the day or week through love or pain.

When you feel centred and peaceful visualise a little seed or acorn in your hands. Gaze upon this miracle which contains all the qualities of that which it will one day become. As you contemplate upon these things visualise the inner light in the seed. Gradually it will shine clearer and brighter and you feel you are being drawn into its light. And you feel you become the seed... Now feel yourself as a seed lying in the deep warm and dark earth. Although it is dark, you feel warm and safe like in a mother's womb. Rest here for a while. Then gradually you will begin to feel a stirring as soft rays of sunlight start calling you. Gradually you feel your roots growing – like stretching your feet deep into the earth. As your roots grow so you will get the power to reach up, up towards the sun. And there you are, your little "head" above the ground. Now the growing flows more easily and your stem becomes tall and your branches reach out and up to worship the glorious sunlight. It is like a song inside you, and then as you feel your branches are almost reaching into the heart of the sun, you burst out in full bloom – like a song of praise and gratitude to the Light, the Creator of all Life.

When you are ready you feel you want to share this love and light, and gradually your blossom changes to fruit or new seeds which you let go of as they fall from you so that others can share of your love offerings, your fruits. Let go with gratitude and ease, knowing that life is eternal and that life is all one and to be shared. Or if you are too eager to share, know that love needs wisdom and discrimination to fulfil itself, then nothing will be wasted.

Then in the full knowing that **all is well** you feel the energy being withdrawn from the leaves and the branches to be preserved in the centre of the plant or tree and in its roots as you prepare yourself for another waiting time, the long rest before a new spring comes… a new creative surge.

Firmly bring yourself back into your everyday consciousness. Feel the chair you are sitting on and be aware of your surroundings, and most of all become firmly rooted in your body. Then visualise a circle of light and protection all around you and see yourself as an equal-sided cross in the circle. Inside you is still the seed of God – always.

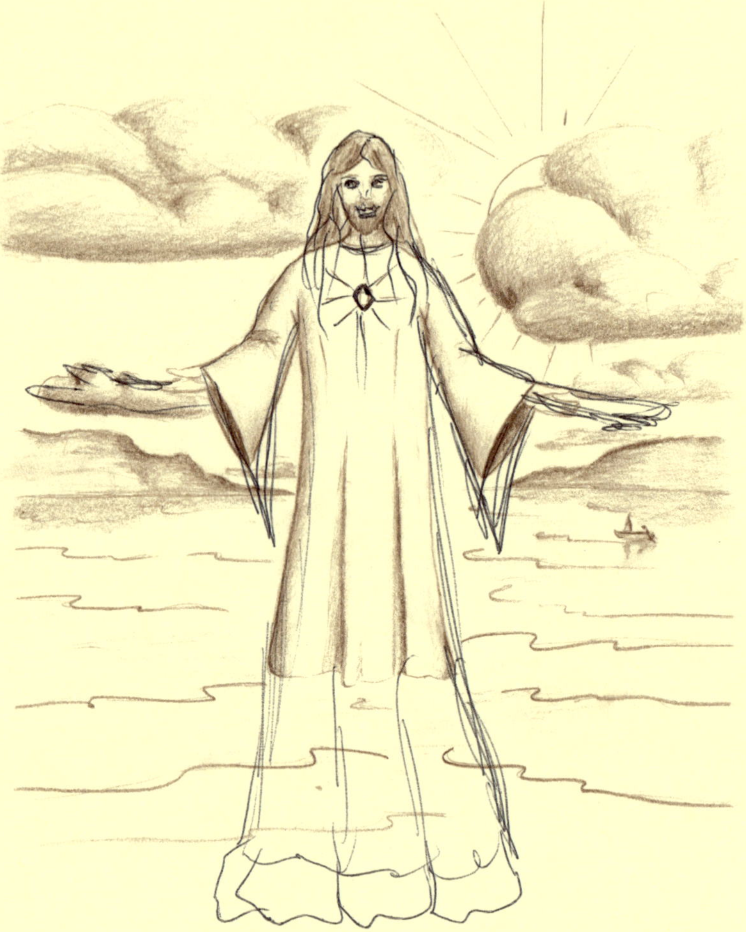

CHAPTER SIX
TESTS ON THE PATH

Those who set out upon the great spiritual adventure must prove their worth. No one can be admitted to the inner circle, or higher mysteries of the Spiritual Life, and be vested with power, until he has overcome himself and certain weaknesses of the flesh.

Henry Thomas Hamblin

Tests and difficulties are something I am sure all our readers are more than familiar with. We meet them all the time just by living in a physical body in a not altogether "perfect" personality which daily has to interact with other "imperfect" personalities in a society full of demands and pressures. Our time of quiet and meditation can for many be a haven (heaven) of peace and relaxation. But as we commit ourselves to a conscious inner life or path, we will also be tested here and tried because this is part of our growth.

In meditation our first difficulty might be in daring to open up and trust that our intuition or "Still Small Voice" is real and not a mere figment of our imagination or is something that we are just "making up". Later, as we advance, we might come up against other subtle tests. We will begin to learn the lesson of discrimination. We may start to receive messages in our quiet times or visions and images. In fact, as we go deeper into the inner life we can have some amazing experiences which may be totally life changing, and almost impossible to put into words as they are felt on such a deep level. If we are not careful and have our feet firmly planted on the earth, we can easily be caught up in illusions set up by our ego.

These deep spiritual experiences can make us feel very special. And yes, we are special in the eyes of God. BUT, SO IS EVERYBODY ELSE! These experiences are accessible to *all* people and a lot of people have them. (Although the wise ones are not likely to talk too much about it.) And even if you have not had them, it does not mean that you are less loved and special to God. It is our spiritual pride that makes us feel we are special, and maybe even a bit better than others. The next step can often be to feel we are one of the "chosen" ones that are exempt from the laws of "ordinary" people. This is of course one of the lessons that we are subject to by the testing powers (which are also of God) because we have to be able to recognise this within ourselves so that we can move beyond the ego. However, the law is clear, there are no short cuts to heaven or divine illumination. We all have to accept and do the work that comes with it! (And in the context I am writing here, we are of course all chosen, the question is: have we chosen God ?!)

If you are in doubt as to what you receive in your meditation or quiet moments is of God/His messengers/your higher self or of the lower self/ego or dark angels whose task it is to test you, I would like to share a few pointers which I have found helpful to remember.

- God or a master soul does not judge or condemn.
- God or a master soul does not play upon your fears.
- God or a master soul would never abuse or interfere with your free will or right to chose.
- God or a master soul does not separate or exclude.
- God or a master soul does not encourage glamour or exalt your ego.

When we have learned to recognise the nature of our lower self, we can more easily recognise these aspects in the religious and spiritual life around us. Today we have a channeller, a clairvoyant, a psychic, a counsellor and a church around every corner. We have all come across the scenarios of personal power. And our spirituality can easily become our new status symbol in the place of materialism or intellectualism. Competition over "who is the most advanced?" can easily take the place of "who has the newest and hottest car?" etc. But we are of course in no position whatsoever to judge that – only God knows. Or if you are "into" guides or reincarnation we hear of all these wonderful famous guides and masters ranging from exalted Kings and priests of Egypt to more famous high masters. And of course most people have at least had one famous incarnation in a previous life! Queen Nefertiti, Joan of Arc and John the Baptist are strangely enough among the most popular! (I do not mean to offend anybody here, but I hope you see that I am merely pointing out the dangers of glamour, not to say what is true or not.)

Spiritual greed is another weakness which makes some people frantically run from one teacher and method to the other in their effort not to miss out on anything. The result is often spiritual indigestion which needs to be sorted out before they can continue on the path. And it is important to find your path as only then can you truly progress.

Another point to remember is that if we are not firmly anchored in our own truth and trust our own light to guide us, we can easily become dependent on someone we think speaks on behalf of God or a master/guide. So it is important to realise that being a discarnate being does not automatically make that being either wise or good. The same applies to ministers of a sect or church; knowledge of the scriptures does not automatically make him/her a wise and good person. We have to learn to be discerning also here in our choice of teacher/counsellor and whom we choose to listen to. Do they teach us to find our own strength, our own inner light and guidance or do they make us depend on them to tell us what to do or to tell us of our worth, how special we are and how loved we are? In return, we give them our devotion and admiration for their insight, and a co-dependent relationship has been formed. A true teacher, encourages you to find the teacher and master within – the voice of God in your heart, the Christ within.

MEDITATION ON HARVEST

When you have prepared yourself for your time of quiet, making sure that you are absolutely comfortable with your back as straight as you can (without being tense) slowly begin to be aware of your breathing – listen to it and for each breath, you draw in that light from the Source of all light until you feel your body vibrant with light. And from your heart you aspire to the highest you know, to the very heart of your Creator.

Gradually become aware of your inner surroundings and use your creative imagination to see yourself standing on a hill top. The air is clear and cool and below, you can see a golden field of corn. It is harvest time The sun is about to set which make the field and the surroundings appear to glow in a golden light.

As we gaze upon this golden world and contemplate the beauty of our gracious Mother Earth, we give thanks to our Heavenly Father, our Creator for all His creation. And as we do so a figure appears to form in the heart of the Sun. God in human form, the Christ Being, comes with His arms outstretched to welcome us into His presence.

And we feel enfolded in Love as we walk towards Him. He gives us the symbols of the corn and the grapes (the bread and the wine), the gifts of LIFE ... Accept in your heart and be filled with Divine abundance of Life eternal ... and become one with Him...

Pause

Gradually come back, but before you do so, for a moment, visualise our beautiful planet bathed in the glorious golden light of the Christ. Healed and beautiful.

Then come firmly back into your earthly consciousness and feel yourself grounded in your body. Then see yourself as an equal sided cross within a circle of light, poised and protected and your heart filled with thankfulness.

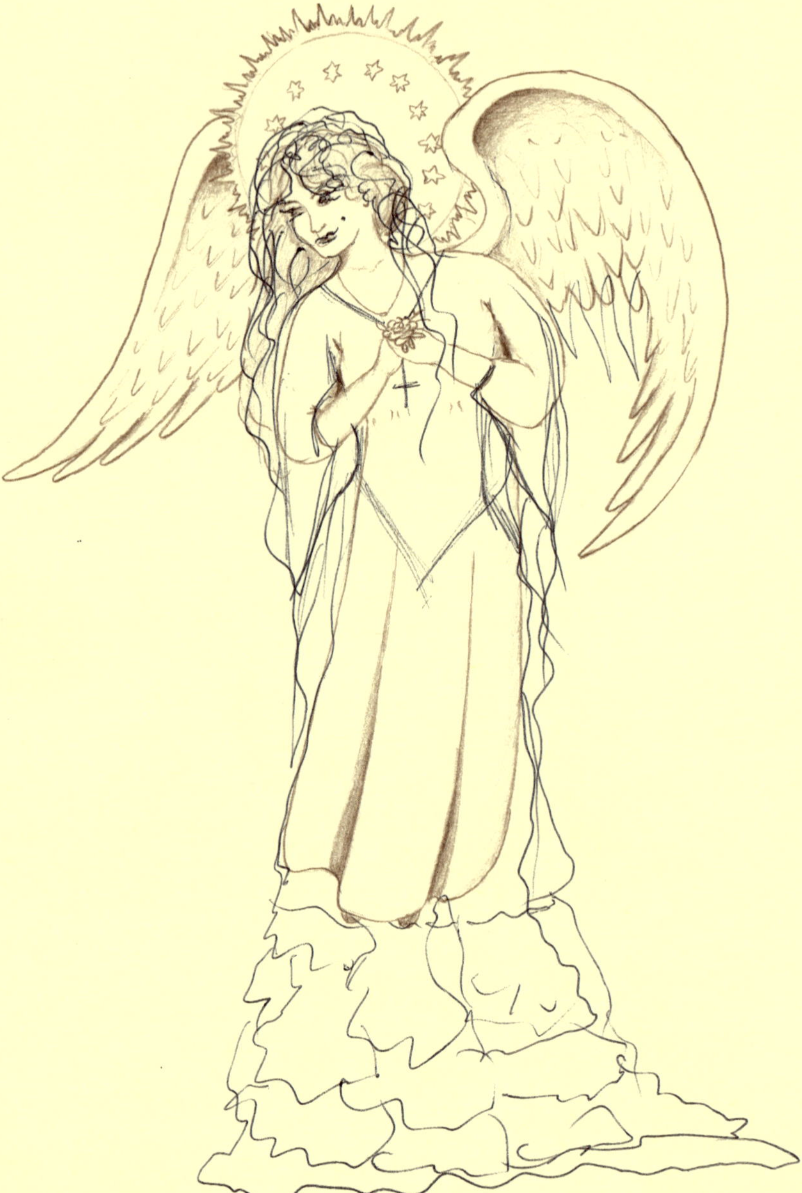

CHAPTER SEVEN
ANGELS & GUARDIANS

ANGELS

Open your heart to the angels.
When you are disturbed in your spirit,
think of the angels of peace.
When you need help to forgive and to understand,
open your heart to the angel of love;
let the angel of wisdom shine through your thoughts.
And on dark days think of the angel of joy,
let the angel of joy bring sunshine
into your heart.

White Eagle

I have found that the awareness of the angels has come to mean more and more to me as I have walked along the path of meditation. Few people may have the experience of angels and many may even have reduced them to fantasy figures which are fine for children's stories and Christmas carols. But the fact is, angels are actually THE theme that all religions have in common. They all talk about them, and our own Bible is full of angel stories.

But what are these beings really? Very simply, it may be easier to say what they are not. They are not human beings. According to most teachings they are developing on a line of evolution separate from ours. We might say parallel with ours. Unlike humans they have no free will, but seem to work very much in full cooperation with Divine law. (Some will say: What about the Dark Angels or "Fallen" Angels? I believe all life comes under Divine Law/God. So they work along cosmic law also.

Much like decomposition is a necessary part of the cycles of nature.) In esoteric tradition the angels are very much connected with the Divine Mother or the feminine aspect of the Godhead. That which creates form, be it soul-matter, mental, etheric or physical matter. So we speak about the angels of music, the angels of colour, the angels of peace, love, joy etc. The angels of nature; the devas and the angels of the elements. The angels which guide the animal races' group soul. The angels of healing, the angels of death, the angels of birth etc – all of which deserves a chapter of their own.

For many of us, and especially when we meditate, our guardian angel is significant. To be able to feel our angel, it is important to remember another aspect which makes them different from us. They do not have emotions. Their love is divine, and can even sometimes be felt as very personal, but it is without passion or emotions. So to contact them – and to make it possible for them to draw close to us – we have to still our emotions and our minds to feel this subtle, yet very real presence with us. In fact tuning into their vibrations can help us greatly in this stilling process.

The following quote is taken from Ylana Hayward's new book on meditation, "A Way to Happiness". She says: "In leading a group meditation, I am often aware of the angel guardian of each individual sitter in the group. At first it appears as if the angel is just behind the sitter, with wings of light outspread; the whole group is within the protective circle of angelic beings. Then gradually, as the work proceeds, it is as though each sitter is at the centre of that being of light which is their angel. Surrounded by and enfolded in light and thus protected from disquieting thoughts and outside influences".

GUARDIAN ANGEL MEDITATION

Let us now invite the angels into our meditation. Even as you listen to your chosen piece of music, you can quietly link in with the wonderful angels of music and colour, and let the notes and the colours flow through you... Then as you breathe in the light from the Christ light or your higher self which is shining above, you gradually become aware of the gentle presence behind you of your guardian angel. Feel its protective loving wings all around you. As your breath becomes deeper and your mind and emotions still, you

will feel that you and your guardian angel seem to be breathing as one – you are one.

Then gently and peacefully aspire to the Highest. See the golden sun pouring its rays down upon you. And as on angels' wings you are lifted up into the golden world of spirit (which is inside you). The Great Angels of the Sun which are playing and dancing in the sun's rays are reaching down to meet you and lift you into the heart of the sun which is the Christ Sun in your own heart. Here you might like to spend some time worshipping at the altar of your innermost being.

PAUSE

When you feel ready, let your guardian angel lead you in your creative visualisation to gently be aware of a beautiful landscape in the world of light – as it leads you down the pathway from your inner golden temple to a beautiful heavenly garden or valley. Here you become aware of the great Angels of Life which are behind all creation of nature. See the teeming life and the beings behind the forms. The tree spirits, the nature spirits – the great devas and the angels of the elements. Feel gratitude for all life and all creatures, and give thanks to the Heavenly Father and the Earthly Mother for sustaining you throughout your life.

Before you firmly ground yourself, let your awareness return to your guardian angel. Be aware of its qualities and thank it for its loyal service. It has always been with you and will never leave you. Knowing that, you will never have to feel that you are alone in your meditation.

Then with feet on earth, head in heaven you stand as the cross of light in the protective circle of light all around you. And the inner knowing that your angel guardian is always watching over you.

THE ANGEL WITHIN

Imagine that an angel lived inside you.
And that every now and then you allowed
Her to look through your eyes.
How different everything would seem.
You would find the rainbow through every grey day.
And amidst each challenge you would see
the golden opportunity within.

Imagine that sometimes you allowed this angel
to direct your feet. She would take you away from familiar
well-worn paths into places
you never imagined you would go.
Each step would be an adventure.
And if she took you towards the things you feared
then you would find the gifts
that had been waiting for you all along.

Imagine that Her angel heart
lay shining within your own.
Every heartbeat would be a blessing and its song
would be the sound of the Cosmic Drum.

Imagine if this angel lived inside you,
how lovely it would be to hear Her words
sounding through your voice,
bringing healing and guidance to all whom you met.
She would bathe in your tears and send them back
in endless bubbles of joy.
You would never feel alone again,
or afraid, or lost. And you would never have to go searching
for answers outside yourself – not ever.

Human brother and sister, the angel in me
greets the bright shining angel in you.

Stephanie Sorréll

GUARDIAN ANGELS AND GUARDIAN SPIRITS

The 'guardian spirit' is a concept that we come across in the Bible and was very much a part of the church's early spiritual teaching. We still find this as part of the Catholic faith, while in other Christian traditions they are hardly talked about at all, neither is the guardian angel. However, in this century and especially the last couple of decades, angels (and fairies) have had their renaissance and also to a lesser degree (although not picked up by the commercial market) so has the idea of guardian spirits. These are more often called guides and spiritual teachers today, and have been brought to our attention mostly through the movement of Spiritualism, but also through New Age related activities where we hear of various people channelling their guides, teachers and even saints or masters. (While in Spiritualism the description of "going into trance" was used when the "guide" spoke through the medium's vocal chords, the medium would rarely remember what was said afterwards. In channelled messages the channeller or medium is usually conscious and therefore aware of what is being said.)

Although it is easier for me personally to "tune into" the angelic vibration, I am also often aware of my guardian spirit or others who come close to me to help and inspire me (called helpers). It can also come as a warm loving presence in a situation when I need it, or it can impress me to say the right thing in a situation. For instance, and I am sure many readers can identify with this, if a friend is in need you find yourself saying the most surprising things that you would not have thought of yourself. Often when this happens people might later refer to it; saying how helpful it was, and you cannot even remember having ever said such a thing. But obviously you did. Alternatively, sometimes it can come as a direct message or teaching like a silent voice within your heart or a sense of knowing, like an intuitive flash where you just know what has been conveyed to you. Most often it can be a more subtle experience. For instance, if you in your meditation ask your guardian spirit for guidance, more often than not our expectations of the right answer may be blocking the very thing we are seeking (or a direct answer might not benefit our spiritual growth), so the answer may come later when we least expect it, as a sudden knowing or simply through a natural course of development in a way that may totally surprise us. And we wonder why on earth we doubted in the first place. I am sure many of you have your own ways of recognising these unseen presences which are unique to you, but which you have developed through your own experience.

The question many people may ask however, is: who are these guides and helpers? And what is the difference between their role and that of the guardian angel? One of the most famous and respected guides or spiritual teachers who has communicated to the world through the mediumship of Grace Cooke is White Eagle. He himself says in the book, *Spiritual Unfoldment I*: "He (your guide) is your companion and teacher, and he works through your higher mind and conscience."

The way to become conscious of this is, according to White Eagle, to learn the magical secret of connecting oneself with the true source of wisdom and, as soon as we can make this connection, we open ourselves to the inflow of the Christ Light, and are able to see and feel the presence of those guiding us from the higher planes. "But it is vitally important", White Eagle explains; "for every soul to make its own effort to aspire. According to his degree of effort man is helped onward and upward by his guide and teacher."

I mentioned helpers earlier. Now, who and what are these? White Eagle explains that they may be spirits or souls that you might have known or are, in some ways, connected to you. The angels who are watching over you, will send them to your aid for a particular purpose and for a limited period of time. These helpers are often likely to be someone you might have helped yourself when that person was on earth. So in the course of your lifetime you may have many different helpers which some clairvoyants may say are your guides, but which in actual fact are not. According to White Eagle and other teachers we have only one teacher and guide who has us in his/her care, and they contact us on a higher level than the helpers often do who, themselves, often manifest on a soul or astral level. White Eagle says of the guide and teacher: "You receive his or her guidance through your conscience, or through the voice of your higher self, sometimes called the voice of God. That still, small voice within can become very strong; it can become for you the voice of your spiritual teacher contacting you on the highest level that you can attain while imprisoned in flesh. All that is lovely and pure will come through from your higher self, and that is the level on which your spiritual teacher works." So we see here the importance of aspiring to the highest we know before we meditate or ask for guidance from our guardians.

Oneferu is the name given by another guardian spirit who used to work with the late Irish mystic, Mona Rolfe. In her book, *Radiation of the Light*, Oneferu says that at one point in our life we are introduced to our teacher by our guardian angel. This teacher, he says, is a Guide, a Being of Light from the world of men (women). "Someone who belongs to one of those great souls of teaching or healing guides, and the power for that teacher's work will mingle in your own aura, so that this colour and vibration will become as familiar to you as your own colour and vibration of light." He describes their presence like a beacon of light that will light up our path as we go forward upon the Path of Truth. He also makes it clear that our guide is appointed by God and are familiar souls that know us maybe better than we know ourselves. They know our failings and our strengths and are there to help us in our service to God.

Our guardian angel, however, has a less "personal" task. It is connected very much with our destiny and has us in its care from the moment we are created and never leaves us. It makes sure that we are lead into the situations we need in order for us to be able to pay our karmic debts or to earn ourselves good karma and be given the opportunities we have earned. Maybe this is why there are so many testimonies of people experiencing their guardian angel saving them from life threatening situations. If you experience being miraculously saved from a fatal car accident, it seems that the 'fatal' outcome of the accident, was not within your karmic pattern at that time, hence your guardian angel's miraculous interference.

Personally, I find it very comforting to know that we are looked after by someone or something that we can even put a name to. However, I do feel it is important not to think of these beings as something that exist outside ourselves, as the danger is that we can be tempted to project our thoughts and feelings onto outside influences and give them our power and hand over the responsibility for our lives to these external beings. My own feeling is that our guardian spirit and our guardian angel are much more closely connected to us than we might think. An American teacher, whom I greatly respect, believes that we are all angels and when I interviewed her on her visit to Norway, she said: "Our guide and master are higher aspects of our self." Maybe the truth lies somewhere in between. White Eagle says in one of his talks; "that our guides are so connected with our higher self that he/she is almost a part of it." Personally I believe that there is a lot for us to discover about the true nature of ourselves and these beings connected with us. The important thing is to remember that to become aware of the influence of our guardians, we need to be still and connect with the highest aspect of ourselves. We must avoid deluding ourselves by playing with the more superficial psychic and occult phenomena of this aspect of reality which, often, can be subject to illusions unless approached with absolute humility and integrity. But stay centered knowing that the gateway to our innermost temple and highest consciousness is *humility* and *simplicity* and the password is LOVE.

Finally some words by White Eagle:

"Your own spiritual teacher and guide knows every aspiration and every difficulty that you endure, and that guide loves you more than you can love yourself."

MEDITATION ON YOUR GUARDIAN SPIRIT

Now relax and make yourself as comfortable as you can and spend some time being aware of your breathing while you draw in the Light from the Source of All Life. As you become quiet in mind and emotions, allow yourself to feel the gentle wings of your guardian angel around you and visualise an archway where the light is pouring through. You feel yourself being gently led through this archway and into a beautiful world of light and beauty. For many of you it may be a beautiful garden, for others it might be a natural site in the woods or in a field of flowers. Whatever it is, use all your senses to create, feel, see, hear and smell your surroundings.

As you walk through your landscape of great beauty, you come to a secluded and sheltered place and you feel you want to stop here. You will find a white seat – a bench or a white stone – where you can sit and rest. Here, you find yourself contemplating the beauty of nature and the wonder of God's creation. Gradually you become aware of a loving presence with you. You are enveloped in a feeling of deep human love and understanding. It is such a familiar feeling, as if you have known this presence through the ages. And indeed you have. Your guardian spirit, your teacher, your guide, whatever name you choose to call him/her is with you and he/she knows you better than you know yourself. There is no judgement, just total acceptance. Open your heart to this influence. If you cannot see him/her, feel the vibration and listen to anything that he/she conveys to you, something that will gradually become familiar to you, something that you will learn to recognise his/her presence by. Or it may be something which is appropriate for your present situation. Do not use your mind or become emotionally excited, just let it flow naturally and peacefully – in humble acceptance.

Pause

When you are ready he/she will take you by the hand and lead you back to the archway. Here, you realise that the love and wisdom and peace of your teacher, who has been appointed to guide you by your Creator, will always be with you. You are never alone.

Then bring yourself back into your everyday consciousness. Take your time, but breathe deeply and feel your body, your surroundings. And when you have grounded yourself, see yourself in a cross of light encircled by light with the protective cloak of God firmly wrapped around you.

CHAPTER EIGHT
USING OUR INNER SENSES TO CREATE

What a lovely month May is in Britain! Every season has its charm, true enough, but there is something about spring which conveys a sense of joy and purity to me. It is the same feeling we experience when we see a beautiful young child uncontaminated by our modern society. And isn't it almost impossible not to feel the rising of the inner sap of life in all of us at this time after the long dark sleep? This inner awakening never ceases to thrill me. Even the colours seem purer and brighter during this time. The beautiful healing spring green, the soothing blues of the forget-me-nots and the bluebells and the bright sun-filled daffodils convey a young vibrancy before summer brings a deeper, more mature settled feeling to nature.

So what has all this to do with meditation? Well, what I really want to convey is the importance of using all our senses in meditation, and spring is the season where most of us are more aware of our senses than at any other time. When we use the technique of creative visualisation it is easy to think that if we cannot visualise anything, we are not doing very well. But as I have mentioned earlier, that is far from the case. Visualisation is only a *tool* to reach that inner sanctuary where we can experience union with God in the silence. But another important point I wanted to emphasise, is that all our physical senses have a counterpart. So when we see with our "inner eyes" we are trying to see and create *form* on a higher spiritual or soul level. People who have these spiritual eyes strongly developed are often called clairvoyant, which does not necessarily mean the ability to see into the future or see somebody's aura as many people seem to believe. That has to do with psychic development which has its place, but does not necessarily have anything to do with spiritual development – although for some these go together. True clairvoyance, however, is the ability to see clearly or to see TRUTH. This is spiritual clairvoyance. The same goes for the sense of hearing. You have people who claim to be clairaudient who can hear voices from discarnate beings or guides etc., but true clairaudience is to be able to hear the voice of God – or to hear truth. Some people complain that they can never see or hear in meditation, yet they can *feel* – an equally important sense. To *feel* the presence of God, or the presence of your guardian angel can be a much deeper and real experience than any vision. As a vision is no good unless *it stirs the heart* – which is actually the purpose of the visualisation technique. Others again can *smell*. In your meditation you may suddenly be aware of the scent of roses or violets or even the earth itself. My teacher says, in fact, that the sense of smell is the highest spiritual sense. It is also said that some of the Great Ones make their presence known to their disciples through the sense of smell. I remember a couple of occasions in our meditation group in Norway where our room was suddenly flooded with the most exquisite scent. And we all felt it. A deeply moving experience.

So when you meditate try to use all your senses. When we activate these higher senses, we give food to our whole being, until we become what we see, feel, hear, smell. In his book *His Wisdom Guiding* Mr. Hamblin says: "In our meditation we can form a picture of a world similar to this present world, but with all its disorders removed, where everything is done for love's sake; where everyone co-operates with everyone else; and where everything comes to pass at the right time, in a perfectly harmonious manner. This is the reverse of day-dreaming; for it is positive and constructive. We fix our attention upon the Eternal Goodness. We persevere in doing this until we FEEL what we are picturing." Eventually we will *become* what we feel and thus manifest God's beauty and love in our outer lives; because the purpose of our lives on earth is for the Spirit of God to use our physical lives for the greater glory of God – to be co-creators with God!

MEDITATION ON DIVINE MOTHER, AND USING OUR SENSES

So after you have gone through your period of preparation using your breathing and/or listening to soft relaxing music, do not forget to aspire towards the Highest you know, asking for God's blessing and guidance for your mediation. And again – feel those gentle loving wings of your guardian angel around you – God's messenger to you. As you feel your mind and your emotions becoming peaceful and still and the sun/star of your higher self shining down upon you, visualise that you stand in front of a white door or gate. The frame seems to be made up from beautiful flowers of your choice. In fact the sheer beauty of the door calls you, and when you look closer you see it is slightly open and that a beautiful light is shining through from the other side.

When you are ready, open the door and enter into the light on the other side. Inside, you find yourself in a beautiful heavenly garden. It is **your** garden. Use **all** your senses as you wander around. **Feel** the green grass under your naked feet. **Feel** the breeze against your skin. **Listen** to the sounds of nature and beyond sound where you may hear the sound of the Universe – the great AUM. **See** and absorb into your being the colours of the flowers, the grass, the trees ... and maybe you will see form behind the physical form. **Smell** the scent of your favourite Spring flowers, the grass and the earth itself. Absorb it into your being... until you feel you ARE the beauty of creation. There is no separation. Creation and you are ONE... *(Take your time in this process.)*

Then in your midst you see the heavenly form of Divine Mother. For some it may be a manifestation of the Mother of Jesus – Mary. For others, She may have no name as we know on Earth. Or you may see Her as a manifestation of Mother Earth – Gaia of the Greeks. Names do not matter, but rather what she radiates to you in the form of beauty and unconditional love. Surrender all your cares to this manifestation of the Mother-God, and know that **all** is well. You, a child of God, are cared for AT ALL TIMES. Remember 'Not a sparrow'... Just BE YOURSELF – there is no judgement, only Love.

PAUSE

When you feel ready, send out your thankfulness in the form of love and light from your heart to all creation. To the animals who *suffer through man's cruelty, to Mother Earth herself who also suffers through man's greed and ignorance, or to any situation which is close to your heart that needs healing.*

Then come firmly back into your everyday consciousness. Feet on earth, head in the sun. The perfectly balanced cross of light encircled by the love and protection of God. You are the cross within the circle.

THE USE OF SCENT AS AN AID IN MEDITATION

I mentioned earlier that the use of our senses is an important factor in meditation and creative visualisation, and that all physical senses have a higher counterpart. Many people may have noticed that during our times of quiet our senses become more enhanced. We become sensitive to noise (a wonderful source of testing your ability in thought control! Yet, not always a welcome one), and if you have been to a group meditation and sat next to a person just back from a garlic meal, or someone who is wearing a very strong perfume of maybe a rather coarse vibration, or even with just a very strong body smell, you will know what I mean when I say it does not exactly help you in your effort to rise in consciousness. So dear readers, do be sensitive to others' needs if you are a member of a meditation group or even if you attend a service! The good news however, is that we can make positive use of scent to enhance our spiritual experiences. The use of incense and scent have always played an important role in rituals and in magic through the ages. This applies even to the Christian Churches themselves. A good way to create a pure scent is to use pure essential oils from plants, trees and flowers, more often known for their use in aromatherapy. These oils are available from most health shops today. For those who are interested in a closer study of these, there are several excellent books available. In this chapter I will just give you a few hints as to the use of some of these for meditation purposes.

The easiest way to use these oils is to buy an oil burner. Most health shops and gift shops will have them. Put a few drops in the water container on top and burn the nightlight underneath. The scent will immediately start to evaporate, filling the room with the desired scent. If you are on your own, the easiest way is to put one or two drops on a tissue which you hold in your hands, or place it somewhere where you can smell it. But remember it is not a question of "the more the better". On the contrary, when you meditate, your senses are very keen, and too strong a scent might be a bit overwhelming and make you nauseous, thus completely defeating the object. This is one of the reasons I recommend essential oils instead of incense for instance, as I personally find it more difficult to find good quality incense and they can often be too much to burn in a small room. But if you are familiar with incenses these, of course, serve exactly the same purpose.

FRANKINCENSE is one of my own favourite oils. It helps us to aspire to the highest we know and opens and deepens our breathing. It gives a wonderful feeling of being in your own space and helps us to feel centred. This feeling of being in our own space gives also a sense of protectiveness. Feeling safe, we relax and can open ourselves to the guidance of our guardian angel and guardian spirit on our journey into our inner sanctuary. This is a good evening oil, but maybe a bit too relaxing if you are tired and need to go to work afterwards in the morning.

SANDALWOOD is another oil that comes from the trees, and is quite a heavy, relaxing oil which works very well at night. Apart from helping to centre yourself it quietens the conscious mind and allows you to enter into contact with the deeper aspects of yourself.

CEDARWOOD was used by the Egyptians and Tibetans as an aid to meditation. It helps us to maintain a sense of balance in our lives. Again a clearing out oil, often used to break up conditions like catarrh, but equally effective in breaking up any mental and emotional clutter and clogged up feeling. Cedarwood should *not* be used during pregnancy.

ROSEWOOD is another favourite of mine from the trees. This oil is more known for its use on social occasions than for use in meditation, as it can create a lovely friendly and light-hearted atmosphere where people are gathered to have a sociable time. However, if you are open to its vibrations it is a wonderful oil that opens not only your heart, but also helps to connect the heart to the crown centre so that you can open yourself to receive the love and wisdom from the Divine. Suitable at all times of the day.

Despite this oil being very inexpensive, I tend to use it sparingly as sadly there has been little replanting of the rosewood tree. So when I use it, I always do so consciously thanking the tree and sending a prayer for its continued existence and growth.

ROSEMARY is an excellent morning meditation oil and a very good cleansing and protective oil. If you feel there has been some unpleasantness in your house which is still lingering, it is a good idea to burn some rosemary before you sit down to meditate or to help the general condition of your home. (Rosemary was in the old days used to clear out evil spirits.) The use of this oil has the same effect on your mental and emotional body, hence it is helpful if you feel you need clarity and clear-sightedness, as well as psychic protection. I have often found it helpful to put a couple of drops of rosemary on my solar plexus (just above the navel) if I know I am going to be in situations where there are a lot of people, or where I know there might be people who are a bit emotionally unbalanced, or even at the cinema, in the supermarket, in the rush hour etc.

If you have a tendency towards high blood pressure or difficulties in sleeping at night I would recommend *juniper* or *pine* as good substitutes since these are less stimulating, but are good cleansers. I would also recommend juniper to those of you who are contact healers or therapists whose work involves touch. Put a drop of juniper on each wrist if you feel you need some extra protection or cleansing properties. (The cleansing effect will also help your client.)

Do not use rosemary during pregnancy or with epilepsy.

CLARY SAGE is excellent to use if you are feeling low, upset, nervous or highly strung. Despite being a stimulating oil, it also helps you to find peace and tranquillity. This peace and tranquillity will help you to see more clearly. I feel clarity is the gift of this oil. It can also be used at any time of the day. But I would warn against this oil if you are on very strong medication. (Although none of the oils work well with alcohol, clary sage in particular could give you an increased effect and a very bad hangover!) Neither should it be used during pregnancy.

The last two oils I am going to mention are two unique oils, unique for their exquisite properties, but also because they are very expensive. To buy the pure essential oil of *neroli* and *rose* may be beyond what most of us can afford, but if you can, it is well worth it. In fact very little of these oils is needed to have an effect, so they can be used very sparingly. However, because of their price they are the only two oils that I would consider buying diluted if I am just going to use them for their fragrance. A diluted oil can in no way replace the pure essential oil's healing property if used for therapeutic purposes.

ROSE has no equals when it comes to its ability to aid in the opening of the heart both on a human and on a spiritual level. In many ways one could say that the rose is God's love manifest in nature. Personally, I also feel its strong connection with the Divine Mother, the feminine aspect of the Trinity. There is peace, comfort, trust and acceptance in the love of the rose which helps us to open up to both receive and to give. And it allows us to touch the Divine in ourselves. Because we feel loved by our Divine Parent we can love ourselves and our fellow creatures.

NEROLI, which is made from orange blossom, has the highest vibration of all the oils, and its gift is absolute purity and peace. There is no oil which can take you out of a stressful situation/vibration like neroli. It brings us in contact with the vibration of our higher self. So whenever you feel battered, shattered, stressed up or worn out, if you can allow the fragrance of neroli to fill you, you will find yourself completely taken out of this state of being and entering a consciousness of absolute peace and rest which can only be found when you are in perfect harmony with your higher self and with God. Even just opening the bottle to inhale its fragrance for a few seconds will help you.

Finally, I would like to make it clear to readers of this book, that my suggestions are only intended as an aid to meditation, and are not meant to replace the work of an aromatherapist, counsellor or medical doctor.

COLOUR ~

When I am writing this the first sign of spring has already manifested. Outside my window I can see snowdrops and crocuses, and the first daffodils are also out. Around the corner I know there are violets. They came out on the 12th of January this year which, for me, is quite amazing. And despite several nights of frost between then and now, they are still there. The signs of small spring green buds are there on the trees and the activity and the song of the birds tells me that spring is here. And when I look at these patches of colour in Bosham House garden, I can feel the hunger in my soul for these colours and how they feed me, and I realise more than ever the need for light and colour at this time of the year when our surroundings have been so dull and grey for such a long time.

However, I have found that we can actually compensate for this lack of colour in our daily life. We can surround ourselves with the colours we hunger for in our homes and with the clothes we wear, or completely free of charge, by using colours in a conscious way in our meditation. I usually start my meditation by breathing in the light, but as light is made up of all the colours we can draw upon one or more of these colours if we so wish. I often find it helpful to call upon the angel(s) of each colour. (As all form has an angelic intelligence that manifests this form, like the angels of music, the angels of peace, the angels of the elements etc., so also with the colours.) If you find this idea or concept strange and unfamiliar to you, it works just as well to think of the colour as an energy – it is the same thing.

There are many books on the market on the meaning and properties of colours, some of them with a slightly different approach and interpretation. I will here just touch upon this vast subject the way I personally perceive it, and leave it to you to create your own experiences.

When you visualise a colour, try to see it as pure and as clear as possible. Use the clear pastel colours and see them as if the light is shining through them, rather than the heavy murky colours which are of a much coarser vibration. Also if you do not find it easy to visualise a colour, think of a flower or a crystal or something else of beauty which has the colour you wish to use and this will help you to connect with that colour's vibration.

RED. Under the category of red we think of all the colours from the deep red connected with passion, to the clear red colour of the blood, representing life and in this connection also of sacrifice – as there is always an element of sacrifice in birth of new life. As we know it is also the colour of Christmas. Red is the colour of love from the pure red of human love to the more rose and pinks associated with unconditional love and the love of Divine Mother. It is interesting that it is realised now that what we traditionally thought of as the primary colour of red (which means that there is no other colour mixed in to make that colour) is in fact not primary red, but red mixed with a hint of yellow. The primary red is more a deep *rose-red* colour. (artist colour: Permanent Rose) So if we feel lonely, hurt or unloved by ourselves, God or others, we can breathe in the rose or pink colours if we need the comfort and healing for the heart or the pure red if we are in need of the more human love. Focusing on the image of the rose which in itself is a symbol of love and the heart will be highly beneficial here.

YELLOW is another of the primary colours. It is often associated with spring, resurrection and rebirth, hence its connection with Easter. Esoterically, yellow is connected with divine intelligence, which is I suppose logical as the mind is what separates us from the other kingdoms of God on this planet. The resurrected human being will express this quality in its perfection. We find it also in Buddhism and the concept of Nirvana, the illumined Buddha reaching the state of pure higher mind free from the wheel of karma and rebirth.

On a more mundane level we can experience how yellow gives us a sun-filled clarity. It is also a colour of happiness, which an uncluttered and carefree mind can give. Because it is mentally stimulating, I would not recommend this as an ideal bedroom colour.

GOLD which is the rather cool yellow mixed with a hint of the warmer pink colour (intelligence mixed with love) gives us what in esoteric tradition is called divine love and wisdom. This is the colour connected with the Christ Spirit, and is also in some traditions the colour of compassion.

ORANGE *(red and yellow)* is very much connected with vitality and creativity, as red is helping to bring the ideas (yellow) into manifestation and physical form. If your life-force runs low and you feel depressed or depleted (often caused by lack of light) orange can be used as a good revitaliser. Use the shade you feel attracted to at that moment, whether a rather reddish orange if you are very depleted physically for instance, or a gentler orange with more yellow in it if you feel your weariness is more of a mental kind. For many, orange is also the colour linked to joy which is interesting as that is one of properties of orange (the fruit) as an essential oil.

BLUE as a primary colour veers more towards turquoise than what we normally think of as blue. Blue is the colour of tranquillity and peace. In some circles it is often named as a healing colour (or even *the* healing colour). Personally I see all the colours as equal in priority as healing colours, especially since true healing is to restore harmony and balance. Healing means to make whole. However, blue is a very calming and inactive, restful colour. So much of our modern dis-eases are caused by over-activity like too much mental work which causes mental stress, strain and emotional upheaval and turmoil, anger and frustration, so we need to calm down and bring some peace and tranquillity into our lives. We need to stop DOING so much and stop TRYING so hard. Blue will help us to bring about a more receptive state of being. This will be reflected in the way we communicate with others, so it is also a colour of communication.

Madonna blue, which is often used in healing, is good to breathe in while we hold our hands clasped over our solar plexus if we feel anxious, fearful or a bit overheated. This colour is found used in connection with the Mother of Jesus, Mary, and is also esoterically the colour of the Divine Feminine manifesting in matter. Esoterically, the colour blue is also connected with devotion and worship.

GREEN marks the balance between the warm and the cold colours. It is the colour of harmony and balance. For many, it is the colour of nature, as so much of the natural countryside, especially in Britain, is green. It is, of course, very much the colour of the plant kingdom, so it speaks to us of abundant life as Mother Earth gives to us in abundance. Green is said to be the true colour of the heart, although some may say that rose is the heart colour. I would rather say that rose is the *healing colour* of the heart as so many of us feel the need for love in our hearts and lives for various reasons. We need rose/pink to restore the natural balance of the heart, so that it can itself express this love. Green is affective where cleansing is needed, both physically, mentally and emotionally.

TURQUOISE which is blue with a hint of yellow is about communication; expressing the feelings of your heart in an intelligent and clear manner. It is a good colour to wear if you are giving a talk, attending a meeting where you need to get your ideas across or sitting an examination. If you have communication difficulties in general, this will help free you up.

PURPLE/VIOLET/INDIGO are all colours which are made up from a combination of blue and red in varying degrees. This is the colour of the highest vibration, and is therefore naturally connected with the spiritual. Although to me all the colours are spiritual – as I even regard the physical as part of the spiritual, so I would rather say that violet/purple is the colour nearest to the part of the colour spectrum which is invisible to the eye (like ultraviolet) These colours are very much connected with transmutation, transformation and change. There is often a need for the sublime and it is a colour connected with the Holy Spirit and also said to be the colour of the energy that is working to initiate the New Age into being. Its role is said to bring our ideas and also spirit into physical manifestation. Being the colour of the Holy Spirit it is, of course, very much a colour of inspiration and wisdom. It helps us to rise above the material and connect us with the divine amidst the hustle and bustle of everyday life. As a transformative colour it is also regarded as a healing colour.

This is also the colour of Advent in the church. Advent, which marks the waiting period before the birth of the Christ Child. So violet is very much a colour of meditation, peace, stillness and also ritual.

WHITE has, of course, all the colours in it, and is the colour of purity and peace. That is also why it is good to use as the soul will absorb whatever it needs from it. Today most people are familiar with the expression "holding people in the light" or "sending out the light" – that is consciously visualising people or places or situations enfolded in light or see them in a ball of light or in a star etc. while you radiate this light from your heart to them/it. This is, I suppose, a modern way of praying for them or the situation. In fact, many believe it to be a more effective technique of healing as it does not impose our ideas on the result according to what we may think. To be good healers, it is important that we remain detached (with love). God's light is sufficient and leaves the outworking to Him. In holding people or situations or countries etc. in the white light or a golden/white light, which brings in a warmth of love and wisdom, is an excellent way to help people **and** yourself.

COLOUR HEALING MEDITATION

When you are comfortable try to let go of all the cares and worries of the outer world and turn your attention inwards to the sanctuary of your soul which is in your heart. Listen to your breathing for a while and feel it become steady and rhythmic and relaxed. Then breathe in the light from the source of Light above you and let yourself be sun-filled as you concentrate your whole being upon God or Good.

Gradually you become aware of a world of pulsating light around you. The love and peace of your guardian angel is with you, and you see a path of colours stretch out in front of you which leads to a brilliant white temple. Your angel leads you gently along the path of colours… You pause as you come to the entrance, and you remind yourself of the password to the temple which is LOVE, and you enter…

... Inside you see that the walls of the temple are in fact not white, but a vibration of all the colours which make up an almost iridescent white, pulsating and vibrating full of LIFE... This is a temple of healing, and your angel leads you to an area in the temple where there are several pools of different coloured water. Let yourself be led to one of these or choose one yourself. Then slowly enter the pool. Absorb the colour you are bathing in. What does it feel like? It might even have a taste or scent? You can float in the water or immerse yourself totally in it. You are safe and you can breathe. Let the colour speak to you or just BE in it.

PAUSE

When your feel ready, let your angel lead you out of the water. (You might be surprised to find that you are not wet!) Then you are shown a seat where you can relax and commune with the angels of healing and the angels of colour. You may also feel the presence of the Great Healer in this temple and His aura seems to permeate the whole atmosphere. Take it in and give thanks for what you have received and feel your heart radiate this thankfulness out to all life in blessing.

Then, when you feel ready, follow the path of colours back the way you came. And gradually become aware of your body and your outer surroundings, gently, but firmly bring yourself right back and ground yourself by feeling your feet firmly on the ground and your "roots" reaching into the earth. Firmly poised, you see yourself as a perfectly balanced cross of light encircled by God's light.

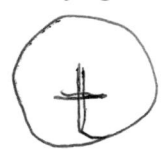

PATH TO THE GREAT SILENCE
A Seneca Indian Colour Meditation

I learned this meditation from a special English lady, Jean LeFevre, who is one of the few white people to be fully initiated as a medicine woman by a North American Indian tribe, the Wolf Clan Medicine Lodge of the Seneca. In 1990, she was appointed a Peace Elder at the Wolf Song gathering. Jean is also now the leader of the White Eagle Lodge of the Americas. The Stepping Stone meditation is based on the teachings of Seneca Grandmother Twylah Nitsch.

I will let the meditation speak for itself as I feel it is not only an exercise in visualising colours and their meaning according to the Indian tradition, but contains a deep wisdom about the journey of the soul towards Union with God. Repeat it regularly and you will discover new aspects of the truth each time you do it.

THE PATH OF PEACE TO THE GREAT SILENCE

Relax and use your deep gentle breathing until you feel a great sense of peace and calm, then we will be ready to commence upon the Path of Peace into the silence. In order to reach the place of peace, we have to cross a river (which to me speaks about crossing the waters of our emotions and sometimes chaotic mind) by walking onto stepping stones of various colours.

*We begin by visualising the first stepping stone in front of us. It is red and we step onto it. It represents the quality of **faith** – and **trust**. We become aware that the first lesson we have to learn when* we are born is that we won't be dropped when someone holds us. We learn to trust that someone will pick us up when we cry, and that everyone who surrounds us is there to help us. While we stand on the red stone we absorb all the good things we associate with faith which we have experienced in life. And those who seek will feel this faith, feel that we are helped in our meditation…

The next stone is the stone of **love**. The colours vibrate from the palest yellow to the deepest gold. Here we become aware of the love that surrounds us. It completely enfolds us and pours into us. We all need to know that we are loved, so feel this love while you stand on the second stepping stone.

When you are ready, step onto the third stone which is blue. It is the stone of **intuition** and **purification.** We feel blue water flooding us and cleansing us from all tiredness, pain and sorrow. Let this purification flood through you, feel it and become one with it…

The middle stone is green. When you are ready, step onto it and try to see the colour with your inner eye – all the shades of nature's many greens. This symbolises the **abundance** which is there to meet our needs – not necessarily our desires or wishes, but most definitely our needs. And when we stand on this stone, we become aware of ourselves, our responsibility to ourselves and to others. We become aware of what we have to give, and what we do…

We arrive at the fifth stone. It consists of all the colours in the most exquisite pastel shades. This is the stone of **creativity**. We take a look at our talents, our gifts. We all have talents, and we begin to see how we can use these gifts creatively. (Do not compare yourself with others)…

The sixth stone is white. This is the stone of **compassion**. The gifts we now carry in our hands we are ready to share with others. As we give we become aware that others are also giving to us. Here we abandon the thought that we are separate from one another, and that God is outside us and separate from us. Here we become aware of the unity of all life – of just BEING.

The last stone has all the shades of amethyst and violet. It is the **healing** stone. Look at it with your inner sight and feel the healing power which fills you and enfolds you. So it is as a healed and whole person you take the next step where you walk into THE GREAT SILENCE – where all must walk alone…

When you are ready – from one minute to one hour, as time does not exist in the real silence – you walk back the same path.

As you return to the last amethyst healing stone, you experience **spiritual healing,** and you become so filled with it that you wish to send it out to all the people you know who are in need or to nations in the world that need healing. Spiritual healing pours out to them…

We reach the sixth white stone of compassion. The compassion we feel is based on **love for all life**. We look around us and see those who have hurt us, but realise that there is nothing to forgive, for we understand, and when we truly understand there is no question of forgiveness…

We have reached the pastel stone of creativity, **spiritual creativity**. If we, on the way up, felt that we did not have any talents, or that we had little to give, we will realise that in the light of spiritual creativity we **all** have something to share. We can read to someone whose eyesight is failing, we can listen. We can think positive thoughts about others instead of negative. We feel the spiritual creativity…

The middle green stone reminds us of nature's abundance, **spiritual abundance** and we feel the need to share not only with each other, but with all life – we are ONE…

*Back to the blue stone, we can now feel the intuition. All that was unclear and which weighed us down at the beginning of our journey is now clear to us. We feel **spiritual intuition** filling us...*

*We are back to the golden stone. We feel the **spiritual love** unite us with all people – breaking down all barriers of separation which teaches us to share. But to share with love...*

*And finally we are back to the red stone, the stone of faith – **spiritual faith** that we will have the courage, the conviction and wisdom we need to go back to our daily life and continue working through its challenges and joys...*

Take your time to adjust to your daily consciousness and make sure that you close well the doors to the inner world behind you, but carrying its wisdom and love in your heart always. Feet on earth, head in heaven (not in the clouds). See yourself as the perfect equal-sided cross within Gods protective circle of light.

CHAPTER NINE
CRYSTALS

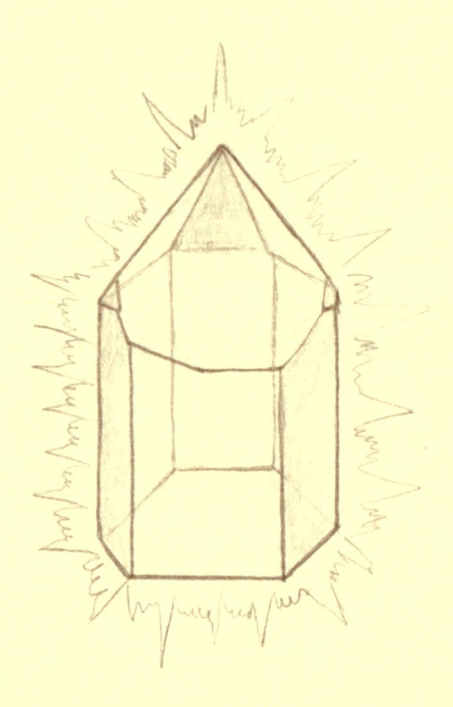

    Over the last decade crystals have become part of our everyday life. They take up quite a large part of the space in so-called "New Age" shops. In many places, we even find specialist shops who deal solely in crystals. Crystal healing is one of the many complimentary therapies on the market. People involved in science and technology encounter them every day, and are in fact dependent on them in their work. Quartz crystals are the basis of the memory capacity in silicon chips used in computers, as it has been discovered that quartz crystals can not only transmit energy, but also have the capacity to receive and store energy. We even use crystals daily to tell the time, as most people today use quartz watches. The chemical name for quartz is *silicon dioxide*.

The above mentioned properties are also one of the reasons why crystals are used in healing, personal growth, development of psychic abilities and meditation. I have often been asked whether it is helpful to meditate with crystals. There is no one answer to this. But if you are not interested in crystals, yet think you "ought to" because it is the thing to do, or think you are missing out if you don't, I am inclined to give the answer: Don't! Crystals are powerful living creations which are neither "good" nor "bad". Like television, it depends on how they are used. Crystals are tools which, like the computers, can be programmed and used in a positive or negative way.

The following personal experiences may throw some light on the subject!

The first incident is rather a lovely one which does not come often in a life time. I had been to a friend's house on a day's workshop on crystals. We had been "feeling" and "tuning into" crystals all day, and being very sensitive to these things I had had more than enough and felt rather "spaced out". It was even with some resistance I accepted holding a very small, rather insignificant quartz crystal my friend brought in from another room. "What do you think of this one?" she asked. When I held it, I was immediately filled with a wonderful feeling of what I can only describe as the pure unconditional love of the Mother. I said: "I feel like I have been welcomed home by a Mother after a long absence, and her love is absolutely unconditional." Tears came to my eyes as I was so moved. My jaw dropped open when my friend told me that the stone was found on top of a

Norwegian mountain, my homeland! I had left my country two years before and, because quite a lot of pain had been involved, I found it difficult to go back still. To me, the little stone became a transmitter or medium for the Spirit of the Norwegian landscape which I love so much. (In Norway we often refer to our country as Mother Norway) The quartz became the link for what I believe to be the great deva of Norway. I felt truly blessed.

The next two stories have a different lesson.

The following incident was of a less pleasant nature. I was spending a few days at some friends' house, and on the first night I could not sleep. I felt restless and my body was tingling all over which made it difficult to relax. The following morning I discovered a huge rose quartz behind the drawn curtains in the bedroom. And the feel of it was not too good. I removed it from the room and slept well throughout the rest of my stay.

The following year the same thing happened, only now I knew about the crystal and could, after realising that the same thing was happening, remove the crystal from the bedroom so I could get a good night's sleep. The owners themselves said that they had never really liked the feel of the crystal and thus it had ended up in the spare bedroom. (It was given to them as a gift.)

Another unpleasant experience which could happen to us all whether we are interested in crystals or not, has a similar message. A friend and I had been on holiday and both bought a gold ring with precious stones. After starting to wear the rings we both gradually began to feel very odd. It was a very spaced out feeling and I felt absolutely exhausted. The same happened to my friend. Intuitively, I felt it had something to do with the stones in the rings. I told my friend to stop wearing her ring until I had cleansed them. My hunch was right, as we both started to recover afterwards. These precious stones that lie in shops indefinitely may be handled by many different people, not just by customers, but by the people responsible for cutting and marketing them. Passed from hand to hand, vibration to vibration, it makes sense to cleanse these crystals of any negative influences they may be storing. Incidentally, after this was done there were no further problems, and we could enjoy the beautiful properties of the precious stones we had each chosen.

This brings me to an important point if you want to work with crystals. Because of their properties to take on and absorb the vibrations of the thoughts and the energy around them, we need to take responsibility for them. If they are loved and cared for, they will radiate that energy. If they are surrounded by negative thoughts and unhealthy environmental energies they will reflect this. This can, of course, be taken advantage of by putting a crystal in an environmentally unhealthy room, like a room that is subject to geopathic stress. The crystal will keep the room healthier by absorbing the negative energy, but needs to be frequently cleansed otherwise the negative energy will accumulate and radiate it back into the room.

In this short chapter I can only provide a few hints to get you started with crystals, if you feel drawn to working with them. I would also advise you to find some good book on the subject if you are really interested. The following guidelines borne from my personal experience might be of interest to you.

1. Start in a simple way and concentrate on one crystal at a time. I would recommend starting with one of the quartz crystals.

2. Choose one that speaks to you, or you feel attracted to. This is the one that is most likely to be right for you at that time.

3. Treat it as a living being. In a way, it is, because it belongs to the mineral kingdom which has its own life force. This life force can be seen through the use of Kirlian photography; which is a photographic technique that shows the aura of a person or object. It can also be detected clairvoyantly as a glow of light around the form. This is an electromagnetic field or aura that surrounds all living matter. Crystals, like all living creations, respond to loving care. It likes sunshine, so try and keep it lying in the sunshine which is often enough to keep it cleansed and free of negative energy. Another way of cleansing it, is to hold it under running cold water. Putting it in a bowl full of salt water over night is another method. For those familiar with Dr. Bach's flower remedies, putting a few drops of Rescue Remedy in your bowl of water is a very effective method. However, you might find that all this takes time and consideration, and the quickest and most sure method once you feel confident about it, is to hold it in your hands and mentally visualise the light cleansing it of all negative energy. With practise and confidence this will only take a few seconds. But if you do not feel sure about it the other methods will do.

4. Another point: be considerate in your use of crystals. When I was more sensitive than I am now, I would often find it quite exhausting to go to people's houses who had lots of crystals lying all over the house. We are all very different and some may be sensitive and responsive to the vibration of crystals. You may on some level, liken it to having to relate to lots of different coloured lights around the room, or listening to several people talking at once. Especially, I find that many crystals in a room while meditating can be distractive rather than helpful, as it takes attention away from the main focus.

I have also noticed that some people can react with a headache or even with a migraine if they spend some time in a room filled with crystals. This is because either the crystals are not cleansed or they have too powerful an effect on that person, releasing too much energy, be it emotional, mental or physical stress which can set off a migraine.

AN INTRODUCTION TO THE QUARTZ CRYSTALS

CLEAR QUARTZ is comprised of silicon dioxide. It is unique in its ability to absorb, store, amplify and transmit energy. The different shapes of quartz crystals have slightly different properties. But it is basically an energy stone and is good to have in a room where you meditate to clear the atmosphere. It is also a good crystal to programme* for specific uses. It has a more masculine feel to it than the softer rose quartz.

ROSE QUARTZ is also silicon dioxide, but derives its rose colour from the additional contents of manganese. As clear quartz is very versatile and can reflect all the colours of the rainbow, rose quartz is, in a way, limited as it is as the name indicated rose in colour by nature, so its use is much more specific. Rose quartz is a heart-stone and related to love which in some ways makes it the safest stone to use in meditation as it helps to open the heart and balances the feelings. An excellent beginner's stone. Wonderful to wear over your heart if you feel lonely and unloved.

AMETHYST is another quartz stone. Here we find traces of iron as well as manganese and titanium which give the reflection of the colour of amethyst. This stone vibrates the highest visible colour of the spectrum and is often thought of as

---

* Programming crystals is outside the scope of this book, and I refer you to many of the excellent books widely available on crystals today at any high street book shop.

the most "spiritual" of the quartz stones as it will stimulate these aspects in ourselves. It also helps us to open up to inspiration. Some people also call it the peace stone which is understandable as peace comes when we can rise above the mundane level and contact our spiritual self. It is known to, in some instances, aid sleep by keeping it by your bedside. (Again I must remind you of cleansing your stone.) For the above mentioned reasons it is also a stone that can help us in times of stress, grief and sadness, and in situations where we need help from a higher source.

CITRINE is a golden to cognac coloured quartz that contains traces of iron. It is rare to find them in their natural state. Most of them are amethysts that have been artificially exposed to extreme heat. Some people feel these are inferior to the natural ones, but whether they are natural or not, they still have many of the same properties. The main quality is that of joy. It is warm and uplifting and helps to stimulate and lift our mental energies to a higher level. It also helps us to have self esteem. This combination makes it a good "exam stone". It is helpful in any "emotional" situation where we need to keep our head clear.

SMOKEY QUARTZ has a pale grey to brown or black colour. It derives its colour from iron and titanium. This stone is said to possess good grounding and protective properties, which of course is a reflection of its grounding qualities. This is an excellent stone to wear after a meditation, or if you find it difficult to be practical and are a bit "up in the air". It is also used to clear blockages and helps cleanse atmospheres.

A CRYSTAL MEDITATION

Relax and leave the worries of your life behind you. Breathe gently and deeply and as you do so feel the light of God filling your whole being.

Gradually you find yourself in a world of light and beauty, and you are gently lead along a path which brings you to a cave in the mountain. From afar you see the light shining through the opening of the cave, and you follow this light which grows brighter and more brilliant as you draw nearer… You enter the cave and you become aware of the dazzling radiance of the thousands of crystals there. But there is one crystal in the centre of the cave that you are attracted to, and it seems to draw you to itself. Observe the colour, the shape and the feel of it… If you are quite still and open your heart to its message – in whatever form it takes – you will receive it into your heart…

Stay with this for as long as you feel you want to, then you can pick up a little miniature version of this bigger crystal and keep it in your heart and bring with you when you leave.

Pause

Then, when you are ready, you walk gently out of the crystal cave and follow the path from the mountain and back to where you came from with the gift of the shining crystal vibrating in your heart. If you want to, you can enjoy the teeming life of the natural world around you before you close the meditation. Try to imagine the energy behind the forms, and feel the oneness with all life, mineral, plant, animal and human – even angelic.

Then bring yourself fully back as described before, and go upon your way with a thankful heart.

CHAPTER TEN
INNER COMMUNION

In the Christian Church we have various sacraments like baptism and Holy Communion. I have never found it easy to relate to these. The fact that the various churches interpret these in different ways has, of course, not helped. Today, when people are encouraged or claim to be able to think for themselves, a belief for instance that a child who hasn't been baptised before it dies will not receive eternal life – or to put it more crudely "will go to Hell" is a concept that most normal, thinking people will not accept; not because they do not believe in God, but because it so obviously goes against the spirit of the teachings of Jesus. Thankfully, this is mostly an outdated belief today. (Note: I am not saying that I do not believe that the ritual of baptism has its place.)

Another ritual that has puzzled me is the Holy Communion. The Roman Catholic Church teaches that the bread and the wine actually become the body and the blood of Jesus during the ritual. The priest partakes in this on behalf of the congregation. For the Protestant, who is given the bread and the wine by the priest, these are symbolic of the body and the blood of Christ. (In some Protestant churches you are not eligible to receive Holy Communion unless you are baptised first.)

In the more mystical traditions the outer circumstances and artefacts are of less importance (although I think most mystics will agree that rituals correctly performed by a priest/priestess or similar who are aware of what they are doing is a very powerful and wonderful act indeed.) For a mystic, however, the inner experience is the most important. A mystic is one who believes that he/she can have direct contact with the Divine; because the Divine lives in him/her, so the need for a middle man (e.g. a priest) takes on a different role. The Holy Communion can be experienced inside you wherever you feel you can enter your inner temple. Also in a church or temple the role of the officiant becomes one of guiding you to enter your inner temple or sanctuary where you can experience (comm)-union with the inner Christ direct.

As you might have guessed, the latter tradition is one that I myself feel in harmony with as it corresponds with my own experiences. However, I want to share with you how I came to have an expanded view and understanding of this ritual.

A few years ago I went on a retreat at one of the Open Centres in Britain. On the same retreat was a priest, and the leader of the retreat asked the priest if she could officiate a Holy Communion. This was an optional activity which most people seemed happy to take part in. I must admit I was a bit unsure about whether it would be right for me, and thought I might spoil the atmosphere if I felt in conflict about it. However, in my morning meditation, a door to my understanding seemed to open and I was reminded that the life and mission of the Master we know as Jesus, was also a cosmic event in the history of this planet. The mystic, Rudolf Steiner and others, talk of the "Mystery of Golgotha" as an event where the Christ Spirit (The Cosmic Christ) through Jesus, poured itself out onto the Earth, so that from that day on the Christ Spirit entered the earth sphere itself. This enables all people to have access to the Christ Spirit if they open themselves to receive it. We now live and breathe in it, almost like the air itself. We and the planet have become part of the Cosmic Body of Christ. Every visible form of life is part of the Cosmic Body of Christ. I believe this is what the Bible talks about when it refers to the reconciliation between man and God through Christ Jesus. And did not Jesus speak of whatever we do to the tiniest creature or lowest person we do unto Him? The Spirit of Christ which is the wine is there for us to partake in whenever we open ourselves to it. The only limitation is what we create ourselves. I realised then that yes, the wine and the bread of the sacraments are the body of Christ (as is the food we eat) as well as symbols, and when we open ourselves in consciousness to receive it, the wine/the Spirit/the Love/the Grace of God can flow into us.

To me, however, this has further implications, as it speaks of the sacredness of all life. God and the Christ are in all visible life which should ideally make each meal a Holy Communion (or eaten in memory of the Christ as Jesus said to His disciples at the last Passover meal), or at least we should remind ourselves that what we eat is part of God and therefore sacred. And by sharing the meal we could make it an act of reminding ourselves of the divinity of each person and the sacredness of all life. Just think of the fundamental effect this awareness would have on the life on this planet if we started to treat each other, the animals, the trees, the plants, the minerals with the reverence the Cosmic Body of Christ deserves! And we find that we come back to the teachings of St. Francis, the teachings of the native peoples like the American Indians, the Buddhists, many loosely described "New Age groups" and other Christian mystics who all share the awareness of THE SACREDNESS OF ALL LIFE. And He who was the channel for this outpouring of Love upon this planet is still working for humanity and comes to give us the Holy Communion in our hearts – the bread and the wine, the Cosmic Body of Christ and His Spirit of Love.

HOLY COMMUNION

Now relax and breathe deeply, but gently as you fill your whole being with light from the Source of Light shining upon you. This light which is there whether you can see it or not because it is part of you, which is in God, in Christ. By focusing on this you are focusing on your divine nature – your higher nature which we so easily cut ourselves off from on this earthly plane, but it does not

mean it is not there. *When you feel peaceful and established in this consciousness (take your time, and if this is all you do, fine!), feel yourself being gently lifted as on invisible angel wings towards a source of pure light. The light becomes gradually stronger until it enfolds you and you are in IT... (Let this be a very gentle gradual process, not a mental brain exercise.) When you feel that you are there, use your creative visualisation or if you prefer : open your inner eyes and see before you a white table or altar. Behind it stands a white shining being – so pure, so gentle and all LOVE. His eyes are full of compassion. On the table before Him is the bread and the wine. He takes the bread and breaks it and gives it to you. Accept it, as you accept your gift of life, with all its trials and sorrows as well as joys and loves. It is all for your spiritual growth and development. Then He gives you the wine, His love, the water of life, His Spirit. Let it fill you and it will give you the strength and the grace to cope and to be able to serve all life according to your capacity. Accept it. This is God's gift to all His children. And remember there is no question of deserving or worthiness at all. It just takes an open heart and a humble spirit.*

PAUSE

Stay with this as long as you feel it is right for you, then gently let yourself be guided back, in your own time, and bring with you this gift and gradually refocus your attention on the everyday surroundings. You might also find it helpful to close with a piece of music and/or a prayer of thanksgiving. Then bring yourself firmly back. Feet on Mother Earth, head in Heaven. See yourself as a cross of light encircled in the light and protection of God. Strong in the Light ...

OUR REAL SELF AND THE KINGDOM OF HEAVEN

> *"The Kingdom of God or Heaven is Divine Union, nothing less. How can we speak about anything so sacred, so wonderful, so sublime, except with bated breath? It is true, although so impossibly wonderful? Nothing less than at-one-ment with God, mystically spoken of as being sons of God, joint heirs with Jesus Christ."*
>
> **Henry Thomas Hamblin**

A reader wrote to me some time ago expressing her appreciation of the Meditation of the Month series, but she had one reservation, she wrote: "I really feel it would be impossible to reach the levels of Christ or Mary in meditation." My immediate response to this was: But we can!

There are two concepts that we need to consider here: First of all to reflect upon what and who we are, namely spiritual beings, sons and daughters of God with the living God inside us. Some call it the God within, others the Christ within, the Christ light, the God seed, the conscience etc., and this concept of God immanent is what all mystics of all religions teach.

The other concept is *The Kingdom of Heaven*, and the various levels of consciousness. We are so used to living in a three dimensional world where time and space separates us from being in contact physically with whatever and whoever we want to be with, that we find it hard to get away from the habitual thought that Heaven is a place "up there", a certain physical distance from us. Or that the various levels of consciousness create a physical step ladder that we climb step by step as we progress spiritually. At the top of the ladder we find Jesus, Buddha etc. with the other lesser saints accordingly down the ladder. But again we need to just go back to the words of Jesus. "The Kingdom of Heaven is within you." And it is actually there all the time within us. We live in it, we breathe in it all the time. It is only our little earthly personality that keeps us separate from it. But when we can contact that Kingdom within, through the Christ in our hearts, we are AT ONE with all life, Jesus, Mary, our next door neighbour (whether we like it or not!), nature, the animal kingdom – the whole of creation really – because here there is no separation, all is one, what we love will immediately be there with us. "In love there can be no separation." And surely Jesus Christ is not confined to the top of some remote mountain where only an elite can reach him. Did he not promise that where two or three are gathered in His name, there He would be? (And this is a most comforting thought because even if we do not feel His presence, He will be there.)

This is where meditation comes in. It is a tool for us to reach that which we are, namely our spiritual self; to get in contact with this son /daughter self which is the real self, which is God. And when we do, we have reached the Kingdom of Heaven because that is where our Christ self lives. Nobody says we will be able to do this each time we sit down to meditate. (Even if all we achieve is a sense of peace, we have done very well indeed); But how can we get there if we do not try, if we do not practise? And few of us can keep that contact for very long when we get there, but having made that contact with our greater self/the *Kingdom of Heaven* for only a second it will have been a transformative experience.

Mr Hamblin says: "The effect of meditation is to change us into the likeness of that upon which we meditate." And for us in the Western Christian tradition, who better is there to meditate upon and aspire towards than Jesus and/or Mary ? For most of us, this is the highest expression of the Divine that we know in a human body. And, if you are one of those people who feel guilty about calling upon God or these Great Ones, thinking they have better things to do than being with you, again remind yourself that your three dimensional thought pattern is limiting the reality of the Kingdom of Heaven and the omnipresence of the Great One.

"Our Lord is still with us to help and sustain by His Spirit. He is transcendent in Heaven, yet He is immanent with us," wrote Henry Thomas Hamblin.

MEDITATION FOR ADVENT AND THE BIRTH OF THE CHRIST CHILD

Now make your usual preparation to still your body, mind and emotions. Slowly and deeply, but effortlessly breathe in the light of God until you feel still and peaceful. It might help you just to gaze on a still flame, using your inner eyes, to quiet the busy outer mind.

We are now approaching the time of Advent*, which is the waiting time – a very still and peaceful awaiting upon the birth of the Christ Child and also for the birth of the new physical light at the Winter Solstice. In the church we see the colour purple/violet applied at this time, so it might be helpful to visualise that you are enfolded in this colour of deep spiritual significance. In this deep sense of peace and waiting we feel our guardian angel standing so close to us, and all is safe. We feel like Mary expecting the birth of Christ. In fact we use this symbol to visualise in our meditation; the beautiful Mother (symbol of the soul) sitting bathed in the light from the Christ (-mass) Star that is shining down upon her (symbol

---

*   This meditation appeared in the Christmas issue of the *Science of Thought Review.*

of the light from the higher self). She is surrounded by many animals (Symbols of the animal nature, also of the humble spirit). But they too are still, they too are awed by the sight. And by her side is Joseph (symbol of the higher mind). We see her bathed in light as the Star seems to come closer and closer until she is in the Star. We then see a beautiful light shining from her heart and gradually the form of a baby emerges from her heart – a golden shining baby...

Like the wise men before us, we kneel and worship Him and we feel love filling our whole being as we receive Him into our hearts. And for a moment we become this baby - resting in the Mother's heart... all light, all love, complete and unconditional...

PAUSE

When you feel ready and before you withdraw in consciousness, be aware for a moment of the light shining in your heart and remind yourself of who and what you really are. And together we pray that we may express more and more this son/daughter of God nature in our everyday life, so that the "Kingdom of Heaven" can truly come to Earth to all creatures. With thankfulness for this realisation, we send out the Christ light from our hearts to all those who suffer and are lonely at this time – and particularly at Christmas – a difficult season for many people. Let us not forget our animal brethren who sadly must endure so much suffering at this time – a time which should be a time of rejoicing for all creatures, high and low. The Birth of Christ – the Birth of the Light!

Now, firmly bring yourself back into your everyday consciousness. Feet on Earth, head in Heaven! The perfectly balanced soul. Like a cross of light in a circle of light. (visualise yourself within this image.)

HOW MYSTICAL EXPERIENCES AND MEDITATION CAN HELP US IN OUR DAILY LIFE

I believe most people agree that meditating is helpful, but apart from making you more relaxed, which in turn will help you to cope better with your day, it might not seem very practical and of much use in that way. So if our time of quiet has to compete with other more important tasks, we often let our meditation yield to those more pressing tasks. After all this "mystical stuff" has nothing to do with real life, has it? Well, Mr Hamblin seemed to think it had everything to do with real life. This was his answer to someone who was too busy doing good deeds to meditate: "My reply is that we can do no good for others if we starve our own soul and neglect our inner life. Our first duty to others is to feed our own soul. We cannot feed the hungry if our own soul is starved and weakened through lack of communion with God. We cannot help others if we do not possess that spiritual power which comes only through quiet waiting upon God in the Secret Place."

To illustrate how this has worked practically in my own life I will share with you two mystical experiences I have had, which in their own way have influenced my life, and are still influencing it, although they happened many years ago. But they are imprinted in my soul forever.

The first one came in my meditation when I was deeply upset. I felt betrayed and hurt. I had lost a lot of money that I had invested, but most of all I felt I was not given the credit I deserved for all the effort I had put into my work. I felt I needed to dare to stand up for myself, which I did, but I still felt resentful angry and hurt. Then as I sat there in my meditation one evening, I was suddenly enveloped in such tender love, and I felt the presence of my spiritual teacher. Then, as in a flash, he revealed his true nature to me. I was absolutely overcome by what I saw and felt. In awe, I just felt like getting down on my knees to worship this being who seemed to me as if the very radiance of the sun was shining through him. But before I got down on my knees (of course he did not want me to worship him!) he changed back to his usual loving, gentle brother self and he just said: "I have only come here to serve." In that very moment I let go of my feelings of resentment. When someone like him could come as a humble servant with no claims for himself; why should I feel the need to claim my "rights" and my "justice"? I told myself to regard what had happened as a service and let it go. I did, and felt at peace.

The other experience was one which actually occurred after a meditation, and we were having a discussion afterwards. I have now forgotten what we talked about, but the experience lives inside me and is part of my soul. In a flash, I was suddenly raised in consciousness and for a few seconds I felt I was one with what I can only describe as the Creative Power of the universe. And in that moment I *knew* that Creation is still happening – it happens all the time. I knew that it happens *despite* us as well as *for* us. And our choice is to go with it and live harmoniously, or we can run in front of it or try to resist it and we end up unhappy. But most of all, Creation goes on no matter what – and most importantly this Creative Power which was expanding and expanding was ALL LOVE. Of course many may say, we know that. Well, I thought I knew too, but it makes such a difference when one has actually experienced it with all one's senses. This is the difference between knowing with your mind, because you have read about it in books you believe to speak the truth and having known it with your mind/soul/body. I believe this kind of knowing is what is meant by faith. These mystical experiences can actually change people's lives and attitudes. Remember St Paul when he was blinded by the light? By practising meditation we become more open to receive these experiences. All the hours we have spent in practise when, perhaps we feel we made very little progress, seem worthwhile. These mystical experiences are written in our spirit and soul forever. I will not say I do not worry anymore or doubt or fear – but the inner knowing is always there: "Underneath are the Everlasting Arms."

THE GRAIL CUP

Now make sure that you are completely comfortable in your physical body. Keep your back straight and chin a little tucked in so that the energies in your spine can flow freely, and imagine that the top of your head is linked by an elastic band to the sun/star of your higher self. Then as usual concentrate for a while upon your quiet, deep breathing. You breathe in the Light of God until your whole

being seems filled with light and love – and you ask for God's guidance and protection in your meditation.

Gradually you become aware of the gentle presence of your guardian angel by your side, and you visualise yourself being led gently up the mountain side. Take your time to get to the top... and be aware of not walking alone. Know your angel guardian is helping you all the way. God never leaves a soul alone. As you approach the top, you feel yourself being drawn into a golden radiance of pure light, filling you and enfolding you. On the mountain top you find yourself kneeling in front of a shining altar – worship here in the centre of your innermost being...

*Then, He comes before you Who is All Love. He holds up the grail cup and bids you to sip. As you drink the Wine of Life, your heart overflows with love and thankfulness. You feel you want to share this love and light with all life. In so doing you **become** all life. All is ONE in God. There is no separation. God is in all and all is in God. ALL LIFE IS ONE.*

PAUSE

When you are ready you descend the mountain side until you reach a beautiful landscape or garden in the valley below. Before you, is laid a white tablecloth set with all the fruits of the earth. As you partake in the food of the earth you know that God will always provide for you what you need (which is not always what you want!). You share with your friends the gifts of Life – also symbolic of your earthly experiences. You share this sustenance with your animal brethren and make a happy communion with all life. Then give thanks to your Father in Heaven and your Earthly Mother for all their gifts.

When you are ready, bring yourself firmly back to your daily consciousness. Feet on Earth. Head in Heaven. And see yourself as a cross of light encircled by light.

CHAPTER ELEVEN
FROM DOING TO BEING

*I sit in the turn of this day.
While the clamour pulls outward,
I spiral softly inwards to the deep
and still of my foetal self.
Light filled. Joy filled.
Here, bathed in innocence,
my soul's cells are nurtured by the Divine.
What richness in this simplicity.
What simplicity in this richness.*

*I look through these eyes and see
the sweeping eyelash of the sky all
filamented in light before the sun's drop.
Yet it isn't I who looks through
these eyes of me.
I feel the presence of something ancient.
Something that knows the very dust of time
held in the bricks and mortar
of these slow houses,
these swelling rocks,
these green bladed fields.*

*In the pulseless pulse of this silence I
am formless, less than mountain air. Yet..
I am infinitely more.
Infinitely all..*

Stephanie Sorréll

When you set your feet upon the path of meditation you might start off believing that your time of quiet is just a period of relaxation that you allow space for every day, not realising that it gradually leads to a totally new way of life, or rather a new *approach* to life. The emphasis moves from DOING to BEING. This sounds boring maybe, but as my mother once said: "People may think my life is very boring, but little do they know about my exciting inner life." Others might again ask: "How do you get anything done if you stop *doing?*" Again it is not so much a matter of ceasing to act, but rather to stop running in front of God or putting spanners in God's works; but rather adjusting one's life to the creative force of the Universe and flow with the creative power of God – which in practise means: *Being in the right place at the right time,* and then acting according to your intuition or to the Divine Will, rather than according to your emotions, your intellect or your instincts. Some call it to "Going with the flow", others; "Achievement without effort". Mr Hamblin speaks about it in his book; *The Life of the Spirit".* I will let him speak:

"There is a deep inner truth which is sometimes hinted at, but is never clearly and plainly expressed in words. It is a truth that is too deep for words or finite definitions. It has sometimes been spoken of as "achievement without effort." The secret was known to Lao Tsze, and today it is engaging some of our greatest minds. They will never solve it through the intellect, but they may do so through intuition. Intuition belongs to the same order as this socialised "achievement without effort."

... There is an inner Divine Order which is the Reality and is always present. Everything that is not Reality has to disappear in the face of Reality. As soon as we leave off striving and resisting, becoming sufficiently quiet and receptive, the

Divine Order appears. It is the Reality and must appear as soon as we become quiet enough. "In quietness... shall be your strength." "Be still and know that I am God." There is an inner realm of quietness to which, when we are sufficiently advanced, we may penetrate. The one who wrote or dictated the 91st Psalm knew all about it. *But this inner secret place of calm is not only a place of safety, it also causes things to come to pass,* in what we may truthfully call a miraculous manner. By miraculous we mean transcending ordinary physical and natural law.

... All that we have to do is just to become quite still and know God. We have not to do anything else. All that is necessary is to let go so completely that our mind becomes as placid as a motionless lake. Just as when a lake is quite still it reflects perfectly the surrounding beauty of hill and sky, so also does our mind when perfectly calm, reflect the beauty, harmony, perfection and order of the Divine. When we become completely still, our mind becomes attuned to the Infinite Mind, after which nothing else matters.

It does not matter how complicated our troubles may be, nor how many or difficult our tasks, if we become quiet, as already described, the whole of our life and work becomes perfectly adjusted. Whatever is discordant "passes in music out of sight". Whatever is complicated becomes simple. Whatever is obscure becomes plain. Whatever seems impossible becomes easy to achieve. No matter how great one's responsibilities, life becomes almost as easy as 'falling off a log.'

... The spiritual life is one long series of paradoxes, and this is one of them. The most difficult thing in the world is to be still, yet it makes life simple and easy. It removes all its cares, solves all its problems, takes away all its fears, relaxes all its strain."

BE STILL AND KNOW THAT I AM GOD

THE STILL LAKE OF PEACE

Now prepare yourself for your time of quiet in your usual manner, then take a few deep breaths and breathe out (loudly if you wish) and empty your lungs completely. As you do so, feel all your cares leave with your breath. Then gradually you fall into your calm, slightly deeper breathing (but remember no strain). Be aware of your breath and listen to its sound and gradually observe the in and out breathing as it finds its own rhythm. You will now feel yourself becoming calmer and more still. Breathe in the Light of God which is above you and around until you are filled with light.

Then visualise yourself by a still lake. Feel your naked feet in the sand, feel the gentle lapping of the water as it caresses your feet. Listen to the sound of the gentle water against your feet and against the shore. Feel the sun warming your skin and see its rays playing on the surface, dancing stars across the water. See the mountains, hills and trees reflecting on the surface.

More and more, you focus on the still reflection of the sun upon the water. All your cares and worries melt away as you just become absorbed in the light and radiance of the sun. You are in the sun.. All is peace... all is well... all is well....... in the sun, BE STILL .... in the sun, in the LIGHT.

Pause

When you are ready, take a few breaths and gently visualise the white carpet of peace being spread across the world. If you can - imagine the angels at work laying down the carpet of peace - especially in the trouble spots of the world. See peace coming to Earth.

As you breathe yourself firmly back into your daily consciousness, try to retain this gentle feeling of peace within your soul as you go about your daily life, and your sheer being in the world will bless people around you. Finally see yourself as a cross of light in a circle of light. Perfectly balanced between heaven and earth. Give thanks for what you have received in your heart.

QUIETNESS VERSUS NEGATIVE PASSIVITY

A question which is in many ways related to the topic I touched upon in the previous pages, *Achievement without Effort*, is the difference between inner quietness and negative passivity. Some people seem to think that meditation is a matter of just emptying oneself and receiving whatever comes in. Or as *some* healers or *some* of today's channellers say: "I just open myself and let spirit come through." That is all very well, but to me that is like, when you want to have a party, opening all the windows and doors and passively sitting there waiting for any passer-by to pop in, hoping you will get on well. But the chance of having unwanted guests arriving is quite high. If we want to have a good time, we make sure we invite the people we want to be with - then after having finished our preparation we can happily await their arrival. It is the same with our time of quiet or any other spiritual service. And here is where the opening aspiration comes in. We aspire to the highest we know in order to link in with the right "guests". In the *Life of the Spirit* Mr Hamblin says:

"It should be pointed out to beginners that the "quietness" which is spoken of in the foregoing chapter is not a negative passivity; but is the result of a reaching up to God. To sink down into a negative, passive state is to descend to the astral plane, and this is accompanied by certain dangers. This wrong quietness must be avoided at all costs. In prayer and meditation the heart and mind must be lifted up until a point of contact with the Divine is reached, and then the "quietness" should be practised. This is being still and knowing God."

He then goes on to explain that this type of stillness is not a stagnant stillness, it is a stillness of "unimpeded activity". He likens it to a wheel; when revolving rapidly it appears to be motionless. I feel it is the same with meditation. At a certain point in our meditation it is as if our conscious effort ceases and the meditation takes its own course without any effort on our part (yet we are in full control). However, this can only happen when the outer self (mind, body and emotions) is absolutely quiet and still. Yet, we are at one with the meditation process which leads us eventually (maybe not every time, or every year!) to that moment of perfect oneness or union with the Divine.

This is why the method of creative visualisation is such a safe and sure method for the active Western mind. It helps to keep unwanted "guests" thoughts out. However, safely anchored in the awareness of God's love and light, always bringing ourselves back to that if our mind and emotions tries to lead us astray, we are perfectly safe. Mind you, do not suppress these unwanted thoughts and feelings, just gently and in a detached manner observe them, focus a few moments on your breathing — then let them go and bring your focus back to that which is the theme for your meditation.

THE FOUNTAIN OF LIFE

So as you prepare yourself for your meditation, make it a special ritual where you are creating room in your soul to receive the Most High Guest. Let your outer ritual reflect this inner feeling of reverence for what is about to take place in your heart. If you do this each time it will become very real to you.

Now, when you have become still in mind and emotion, and your body feels as comfortable as you can make it, lift your heart to the Most High. Personally, I find visualising a sun or star helpful and let yourself be bathed in the light that is shining down upon you. Just let your heart's feeling express your aspiration to become one with the ONE and for His light to guide you in your meditation.

Firmly centred in this light use your power of imagination and see yourself in a beautiful sunlit spring landscape. Use your senses to become aware of the activity in nature at this time. See the beautiful sunlit spring green (such a healing colour) all around you. Hear the sound of nature's feathered orchestra accompanied by the rustle of leaves and singing brook. Feel the upsurge of nature's energy at this time like a wonderful choir praising God and the glorious awakening in nature.

Then, in front of you, see and hear a fountain of spring water coming up from the ground. Where the sunlight meets the water it creates rays of iridescent rainbow light. You feel drawn to it and step into the fine shower of rainbow water – so healing and cleansing. Gradually you become aware of a human form in the fountain and you realise that you are in the aura of the Great Healer – the Master. And if you listen deep within your heart, you will hear the words, I AM the water (spirit) of life – I AM the resurrection and the Life. I AM – I AM – I AM… And He gives you His cup of liquid rainbow to drink. As you partake in this communion you realise that the voice is the voice of God within you – the Son of God in you – the I AM …

PAUSE

When you are ready, slowly go back the way you came through the landscape. And now feel that there is no separation between you and nature; you and the animals; you and your human brothers – or angelic brethren. We all belong to the Great Symphony of Life. And in this feeling of oneness with all life, let light and healing go out to any situation you know needs it. Then bring yourself firmly back to your physical everyday consciousness. Become fully grounded and see yourself as a cross of light encircled by light for protection. Then go upon your way with a song of thankfulness in your heart.

CHAPTER TWELVE
SOUNDING OUR TRUE NOTE

Our true life is really like the graceful flight of a bird, or the dancing of insects in the sunlight. Instead of being dull and heavy, we should be light, like a bird on the wing, or thistledown borne on the gentle breeze. We are far too serious. I firmly believe that there is laughter in Heaven, a joyous expression of infinite joy.

Henry Thomas Hamblin

Have you ever thought of yourself as a bird and asked yourself: "I wonder what my song would sound like?" I believe that like the bird we all have a song inside us which is uniquely ours. I do not mean this in an abstract, symbolic way, but in a very real way. Science today recognises that all life has a vibration, and all vibration has a note. Although that note is not within the frequency that our physical vehicle can recognise as what we call sound , it does not mean that the sound does not exist. The Bible itself talks about the beginning of creation as the Word. "In the beginning was the Word ...." The Word/the Logos which took human form in its fullness through Jesus, so that we could recognise our own potential divinity, as that same light/word shines in us all. So in a way you could say that the song in you and your light is another expression of the same truth. However, as we cannot hold the full power of the creative Word of the Universe or even of humanity as a whole, we are an expression or an aspect of the whole of humanity – like one of the notes in a symphony. This brings me back to the point of this article which is the importance of being true to your own note or song. If not, the symphony will not sound right. And to be honest the collective human orchestra does not seem very harmonious at the moment.

I went to a talk some time ago, and the speaker, Simon Bentley, gave a very good example from a seminar he had attended. Several people were asked to read the same inspirational text out loud. What struck him was that although the text was beautifully read by all, he noticed that each person seemed to bring out slightly different aspects of truth from this text of inspirational teaching.

He realised that this came from their own being. From one he received the *strength* contained in the text. From another it was the quality of *love*, from another it was the quality of *peace*, from another the quality of *truth* etc. Because it was the teaching of a master soul they could not express the totality of the text of course, but they could express the aspect which was in tune with their own note. So again we come back to the question: What is our own note? Which note am I born to express in this life? Do I try to sing the song of my neighbour whom I admire or envy and so fail my own? The following poem seems to illustrate these points so well.

On Being Yourself

You must learn that you may not be loved by all people.

You can be the finest apple in the world – ripe, juicy,

sweet, succulent and offer yourself to all.

But you must remember that there will be people

who do not like apples.

You must understand that if you are the world's finest apple,

and someone you love does not like apples, you have a choice

of becoming a banana.

But, be warned, if you choose to become a banana,

you will be a second-rate banana.

Remember, you will always be the finest apple.

You must also realise that if you choose to become a second-rate banana,

there will be people who do not like bananas.

Furthermore, you can spend your life trying to become

the best banana – which is impossible if you are an apple –

or you can seek again to be the finest apple.

Author Unknown

Here, we can recognise ourselves perhaps! Am I an apple trying to be a banana because I am the only apple in the bowl of fruit – and consequently totally failing to be a perfect apple? Am I one of those who ruin the symphony because I sound the wrong/discordant note? I bet most of us feel like the apple – being an oddball. Our upbringing may have taught us that a banana is the thing to be in this world. However, life has been teaching me more and more lately that life is not so much a question of purpose and goals as it is about BEING – it is about sounding our note in *all* that we do. *What* we do is secondary, and our purpose will unfold naturally, from there.

But how can we find this note? Again it is not so much a question of going on a quest as to *stop trying*. Let go. Be still. It is in the stillness that you will come in touch with your true note. If you can contact this note in the stillness every day, you will gradually find that you will express this note in your life more and more. Yes, it will even make you feel uncomfortable if you do not, even painful. So if you feel pain or dissatisfaction, ask yourself: Is it because I am not sounding my note, singing my song?

Mr Hamblin says: "Indeed, we discover that we are the very things we express, in much the same way that the picture that an artist paints is part of himself and is an expression of himself. If he did not possess the beauty within him he could not express it; if he were not the very spirit of beauty itself he could not portray beauty on his canvas."

Let our prayer be:

LORD, HELP ME TO SING MY SONG.

THE CREATIVE SOUND OF LIFE

When you have made yourself as comfortable as you can, just let all your worries and cares drop away from you. As you breathe in God's light from the source of light above you (which is also inside you), feel as you breathe out all mental clutter dropping away from your forehead and let your mind gently sink into the consciousness of your heart. For a few moments just concentrate on your breathing and you will feel that gradually your emotions will quieten too. Draw the light in more and more until you feel sunfilled, light and peaceful, knowing that God is Omnipresent and your guardian angel is at your side.

Now visualise yourself standing in a beautiful snowy landscape at dawn. It is so still. Nature rests under the soft white carpet of white snow. But gradually you will hear that underlying the silence is a sound; very faint at first, but as the strings of your heart slowly start to resonate with the stillness you might become aware of the sound of creation, the great Aum/Om – a vibration rather than a sound.

As you start to experience this you also become aware of the soft golden glow on the horizon, and soon the rays of the rising sun will start playing on the glittering snow, covering it with a million jewels. Without losing touch with the vibration in your heart, you become aware of nature's sound around you as it wakes up to a new day. You are aware of the sound of the birds and the gentle breeze in the trees. But most of all you feel your own heart's stirring, and a song rises within you as you give thanks and praise your Creator for the gift of life. Feel the sense of freedom this gives you and let your spirit rise like a bird and fly into the Sun – the Source of your life – the "I AM" in you which is of God, in God. Let yourself be absorbed into this Light.

PAUSE

When you feel ready, gradually breathe yourself down and before you totally re-enter your everyday consciousness, again see yourself standing in the pure white winter landscape and contemplate.

You might contemplate the time ahead or the nature of your song. Just let whatever comes to you be received in peace and without judgement or interference from the analytical mind. Listen, with your heart ...

Then give thanks and send light and healing from your heart to that which you feel is close to your heart and may need it. Then make yourself come firmly into your everyday consciousness. Feel your body and your physical surroundings. Let that light above and in you reach deep into the soil of the earth, like the roots of the tree. Then see yourself as a cross of light in a circle of God's protective light.

THE END

EPILOGUE

INNER TEMPLE

*Dear Friend, remember that you carry
a treasure within you that was yours
even before you were born.
It was there as you grew within the womb.
It will be with you until you depart from this world
and after ...
Really, it is the only thing you will ever possess.
It is priceless because wherever you go
or whatever you do it will never leave you or diminish with age.
In fact as your need grows,
it will become more valuable.
Although your life may take you to many holy places;
churches, mosques, shrines
they will never compare with this within you.
For it is a temple of the Spirit which will free
you from any sense of imprisonment, illness
or loneliness.
The only problem, Dear Friend, is that you might forget
this and go searching for this same temple elsewhere.
Great will be your despair and frustration until
you trace the path back to the steps of your own soul.*

Stephanie Sorréll

SCIENCE OF THOUGHT REVIEW

Founded in 1921 by the late Henry Thomas Hamblin, a practical English mystic, and presently edited by Stephanie Sorréll, this bi-monthly, charitable magazine is devoted to the spiritual life and applied thinking.

The underlying theme of the SCIENCE OF THOUGHT REVIEW is based on a greater understanding of our spiritual centre of identity, and instructive, helpful guidelines are given to enable us to apply this greater understanding to our everyday life. The steadfast practise of this teaching can transform our life and has done so in countless individuals for over 70 years.

The magazine is not an attempt to establish a new cult or religion, but rather a sincere effort to help people of all shades of religious belief (or none), on their transformative, spiritual journey. It meets a real need in the hearts and minds of many who are seeking for a deeper meaning to life and inner stability. Its precepts can be read and practised by anyone. The emphasis is not so much on belief but rather on personal spiritual experience, as the articles and poems by its contributors indicate.

The SCIENCE OF THOUGHT REVIEW has a large circulation and goes to a multitude of peoples in many walks of life all over the world, many of whom find it provides a "life line" through difficult and troubled times. It is published at a price that is much less than the cost of production and distribution, so as to bring it within reach of all. It is subsidised, however, by the kindness and loyal support of readers who are in a position to give more than the minimum subscription asked.

RECOMMENDED READING

From: **THE SCIENCE OF THOUGHT PRESS LTD.**
Bosham House
Bosham
Chichester
West Sussex PO18 8PJ England

THE RIVER THAT KNOWS THE WAY edited by Stephanie Sorréll (ISBN 0-9531597-0-1)

LIFE OF THE SPIRIT by Henry Thomas Hamblin

HIS WISDOM GUIDING by Henry Thomas Hamblin (edited by Clare Cameron)

WITHIN YOU IS THE POWER
by Henry Thomas Hamblin

GOD OUR CENTRE AND SOURCE
by Henry Thomas Hamblin

From: **THE WHITE EAGLE PUBLISHING TRUST**
New Lands
Rake, Liss
Hampshire GU33 7HY England

A WAY TO HAPPINESS by Ylana Hayward
(ISBN 0-85487-094-6)

MEDITATION by Grace Cooke (ISBN 0-85487-059-8)

THE JEWEL IN THE LOTUS (ISBN 0-85487-067-9)

THE STILL VOICE by White Eagle (ISBN 0-85487-049-0)

SPIRITUAL UNFOLDMENT I by White Eagle
(ISBN 0-85487-012-1)

SPIRITUAL UNFOLMENT II by White Eagle
(ISBN 0-85487-075-X)

From: **HODDER & STOUGHTON**
338 Euston Road
London NW1 3BH
England

EMISSARY OF LIGHT by James F. Twyman
(ISBN 0-340-69645-1)

From: **THE C.W. DANIEL COMPANY LTD**
1 Church Path
Saffron Walden
Essex CB1O 1JP, England

SUBTLE AROMATHERAPY by Patrica Davis
(ISBN 0-85207-227-9)

From: **HARPER COLLINS PUBLISHERS LTD**
77-85 Fulham Palace Road
Hammersmith
London W6 8JB, England

THE MAGIC OF CRYSTALS by Wendy Jones & Barry Jones (ISBN 0-7322-5714-X)

From: **JUDY PIATKUS PUBLISHERS LTD**
5 Windmill Street
London W1P 1HF, England

THE POWER OF GEMS AND CRYSTALS by Soozi Holbeche (ISBN 0-86188-954-1)